The Lost City of
EXETER
– Revisited

Chips Barber

Sally Barber

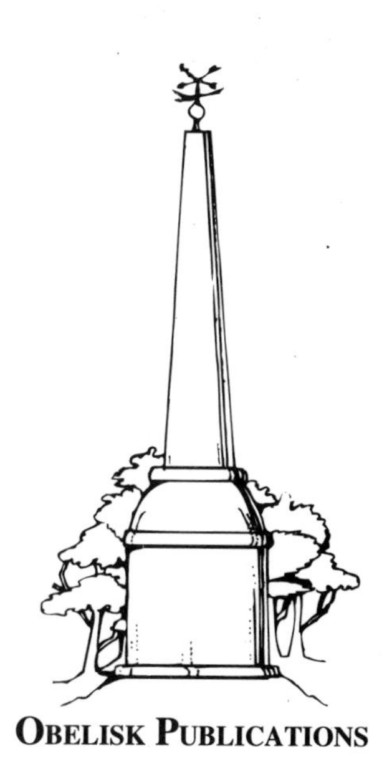

OBELISK PUBLICATIONS

Also By The Author

Around & About the Haldon Hills – Revisited
Diary of a Dartmoor Walker
*The Torbay Book**
Diary of a Devonshire Walker
The Great Little Dartmoor Book
The Great Little Exeter Book
*DevonAir Book of Family Walks**
Made in Devon
*Dartmoor in Colour**
Burgh Island and Bigbury Bay
Dark & Dastardly Dartmoor
*Exeter in Colour**
Torbay in Colour
Ghosts of Exeter
The Great Little Totnes Book
Tales of the Teign
Ten Family Walks on Dartmoor
The Great Little Plymouth Book
Plymouth in Colour
Weird & Wonderful Dartmoor
Ghastly & Ghostly Devon
Dawlish and Dawlish Warren
The South Hams
Torquay / Paignton / Brixham
Ten Family Walks in East Devon
Around & About Salcombe
Around & About Seaton
Around & About Sidmouth
Around & About Teignmouth and Shaldon
Chudleigh Collection
Brixham Album
Topsham Past and Present
Beautiful Dartmoor
From The Dart to The Start
Dartmouth and Kingswear
Cranmere Pool – The First Dartmoor Letterbox
The Great Little Chagford Book
The Teign Valley of Yesteryear Parts I and II
Brixham of Yesteryear Parts I, II, III
Pinhoe of Yesteryear Parts I and II
Haunted Pubs in Devon
Princetown of Yesteryear Parts I and II
The South Hams in Colour
Six Short Pub Walks on Dartmoor
Torbay in Colour – Torquay Paignton Brixham
Widecombe – A Visitor's Guide
Newton Ferrers & Noss Mayo
Along The Otter
Colourful Cockington
Heavitree of Yesteryear
Railways on and around Dartmoor
Sidmouth Past and Present
Walks on and around Woodbury Common

**titles no longer available*

Acknowledgements

My thanks are due to the many people who kindly helped me in the preparation of both the original version and revised edition of this book. Sadly a number of them have passed away in the intervening years and these include the following who provided photos: Charles Radley, George Parsons, Tom Higgins, Harold Stringer and Mike Williams. Many of the old picture postcards are from the collection of Tom Higgins and my thanks are extended to Julia Higgins for very kindly allowing me to use them. Mrs Fitzjohn also very kindly allowed me to dip into the family albums of Charles Radley. I would also like to thank the following for their contributions: John Bartlett, Dave Barrett, Sandra Barrett, The Exeter St Thomas Cricket Club, Ian Jubb, Mavis Piller, Mike Williams; and Jane Reynolds for the drawing on page 88. All other pictures were taken or collected by myself.

First published in 1982 (0 946651 02 7), Reprinted in 1983, 1985 and 1989
Revised edition (1 899073 61 2) published in 1998 by
Obelisk Publications, 2 Church Hill, Pinhoe, Exeter, Devon
Designed by Chips and Sally Barber
Printed in Great Britain by

CONTENTS

Introduction

The original version of this book was first published at the end of 1982 and followed hard on the heels of *Around & About the Haldon Hills*. The years have rolled quickly, and alarmingly, by since then and my literary travels around Devon have taken me to many wonderful places and into many people's houses in the process of compiling many more books. However, places and circumstances have gradually changed in my native Exeter and even more has been 'Lost' in our lovely city since 1982. This revamped edition seeks to update the 'story', at least for the time being. Fortunately much of the city's history remains unchanged as we look first at the central area of the city, the parts which most visitors get to see.

The Heart of Exeter

The Romans developed it, the ancient British let it decay, the Danes burned and plundered it, the Normans besieged it, the Georgians and Victorians extended it, the Germans blitzed it and we, for the most part, cherish it. The Heart of Exeter, apart from occasional murmurings, survives as the area of the City principally blessed with many treasures of historic value; here are just some of them.

The Cathedral Precincts

There is an air of reverence about this marvellous corner of Exeter. Within the precinct many people come to admire the Cathedral – old hands who have seen it many times merely make the pilgrimage to the Cathedral Green to keep the building company, and to eat their sandwiches! On hot summer days the white statue of Richard Hooker, historian, presides over all manner of activities which range from very English Morris dancers to courting couples. Hooker keeps an extremely wistful expression, and well he might with the pigeons of the yard enjoying rich pickings from leftover lunches and titbits before flying menacingly around his head. Many visitors continually click their cameras at ancient buildings like 'Mol's Coffee House' but their main subject is the principal edifice that everyone associates with Exeter.

The Cathedral

Exeter has been a Cathedral City since 1050 when Leofric, the Bishop of Crediton, was granted permission by Edward the Confessor to change the Bishop's 'stool' from Crediton to Exeter.

In the middle of the thirteenth century Bishop Walter Bronescombe, also known as Walter the Good (he was allegedly crafty and mean), developed many of the buildings and layout, much as they are seen today. He restored the Lady Chapel and was later buried in it. His successor was the famous Bishop Peter Quivil (or Quinil) who continued the development of the buildings but constantly annoyed the Franciscans. The Divine Hand of Fate saw him die on the eve of the Feast of St Francis!

In the North Transept is the Cathedral clock, believed to be one of only four of its type in England. It is more than 600 years old, which may account for its geographical inexactitude. In the centre of its face is the earth; the moon travels around it, and waxes and wanes by the inner point of a fleur-de-lis marked by a pointer. The hours are revealed by the outer point but it was not until 1760 that minutes were shown. Its Latin motto means 'They pass by and are reckoned up'. It is thought that the clock was made by Peter Lightfoot, a monk of Glastonbury Abbey; if this is the case it would date the clock to about 1376.

The great bell called Peter, one of the biggest in the country, is above the clock high in the north tower. Bishop Courtenay had it brought from Llandaff in the fifteenth century – this must have been quite a feat as it weighs $5\frac{1}{4}$ tons. In 1611 it was cracked due to a 'too violent ringing in commemoration of the Gunpowder Plot'. A pub that once existed between the Cathedral and Palace Gate was called 'The Peter Bell' but was pulled down in 1811 to enable the road to be widened.

The Cathedral is well documented by a host of other writers and those keen to know more about it can also enjoy a guided tour.

Richard Hooker's Statue

In the Green the 'pious' Richard Hooker sits sentinel in front of the Cathedral. The 'Judicious Hooker' was born in Heavitree in 1554 and was the author of *Ecclesiastical Polity*. Apparently he was a slovenly fellow who was devoid of pulpit graces, and he even permitted his landlady, Mrs Churchman, to find him a wife. Her choice was her own bullying daughter. Whilst Hooker contemplated how best to rule the ecclesiastical world, his wife, Joan, described as 'an ill-bred, bad-tempered girl, neither rich nor beautiful', made him rock the baby's cradle.

In his life, which spanned just 47 years, he travelled the country and with his radical thinking proved a controversial figure in religious circles. His last years were spent near Canterbury but he died in Bishopsbourne near Canterbury, just a short time before his wife.

Hooker's statue serenely sits, surrounded by shrubs, on the Cathedral Green. This now most pleasant of patches was once the common burial place for Exeter citizens until 1636. The accumulation of corpses and burial mounds was an obvious health risk and threatened to bury the Cathedral! As a result the Bartholomew Street cemetery to the west, against the city wall, was opened in 1637.

Mol's Coffee House

This is a most distinctive, frequently photographed, Elizabethan building on the eastern side of the Close. At the time of the Armada it was a private dwelling which entertained both Francis Drake and Walter Raleigh. When coffee was introduced into England it was opened as a 'Club and Coffee House' by an Italian called Mol. It remained popular with local dignitaries until 1829. In an upstairs area is a fine panelled room which bears the arms of many past famous Devon families. The ground floor is occupied by the stationer and map specialist, Eland's, a long-established name in Exeter.

The Royal Clarence

'Comfort blended with antiquity' is how the Royal Clarence saw itself in the 1920s, and little seems to have changed. Established in 1769, 'The Hotel', as it was called, was believed to be the first in England to use the French word 'hotel' in its name. In its early years it saw many landlords come and go, each giving their names to the establishment, such as Thompson's and Phillips' Hotel.

The idyllic setting of the hotel, overlooking Exeter's splendid Cathedral, was an asset in attracting a clientèle of great standing. The Duke of Kent, son of George III and father of Queen Victoria, was reputedly brought to the hotel after he died in Sidmouth on 23 January 1820 and laid to rest in the room they call 'the Unicorn'. Arrangements were made with Mr Clench of the New London Inn to supply the hearses, horses and coaches for the cortège and its sombre journey to Windsor.

An earlier visitor was Lord Nelson who arrived complete with two good arms on 15 January 1801. He gave a reception for 'most of the respectable inhabitants' of Exeter. In a book about the history of the Royal Clarence there is a copy specimen signature given by Nelson with his right hand before it was lost, and of the left hand shortly afterwards.

The Royal Clarence gets its name from the visit of the Duchess of Clarence on 13 July 1827 whilst on her way to join the Duke at Plymouth. No doubt she enjoyed good 'fayre' as the hotel had built a fine reputation. Nearly a century later, in a paper called the *Winning Post*, this further appreciation was rendered:

"So we slipped into Exeter for a stroll round the shops and lunch at the Royal Clarence – lovely lobsters from the coast, lamb from local pastures, junket and Devonshire cream, Stilton, and Jubilee Port. Why go on? But we had to, bidding our best friend, the headwaiter, a tearful goodbye."

According to one senior citizen it was not possible for the police to arrest a person for being drunk at the Royal Clarence or the Globe. To maintain order the landlord had to make haste to the Cathedral and summon the verger who was empowered to take the inebriated fellow back to the Cathedral until he or she was sober again. This seems to be because the Royal Clarence is sited on ecclesiastical ground and outside of the law for certain offences. The Globe stood at the South Street end of the Cathedral Yard and was a victim of the blitz.

The Ship Inn (Martin's Lane)

Historically the Ship Inn has had a most colourful past. Reputed visitors include those great Elizabethan seamen Raleigh, Hawkins, Grenville and, of course, Sir Francis Drake. The latter is alleged to have written in a letter dated 1587: "Next to mine own shippe I do most love that old 'shippe' in Exon, a tavern in Fysh Street, as the people call it or as the clergie will have it St Martin's Lane. There yester'en I had some speech with a mariner fresh come hither from Plymouth … The power of Spain is already afloat, so in the morning please God, I am for Plymouth and for another Shippe than this."

On one occasion when Drake adjourned to the Ship by himself he is believed to have been thrown out for being drunk and from that time on he always went there accompanied. His drunken antics have nothing to do with the fact that the 'St' has been dropped from the name of the lane because the same has happened to Mary Arches Street, Catherine Street and Paul Street.

Martin's Lane has also been called 'Luxury Lane' in the past. Formerly it was a cobbled thoroughfare with a centre drain which accepted some unpleasant discharges. Frequently stage coaches passed along it, presumably straddling the drain. During the Civil War (1642–1646) Captain Benet, a Royalist, billeted his troops there whilst the city was being besieged by General Fairfax. In a letter to his commanding officer, dated 1644, he stated:

"I have quartered my men at the Ship in St Martin's Lane, an excellent place with good wine, victual and forage."

Nothing would appear to have changed, except for a new clientèle! In 1719 the Ship was threatened by a mob intent on burning it down because they thought the clergy, with an allegiance to the Whig Government, were being sheltered there. A vigilant group of soldiers fortunately broke up the mob.

The Guildhall and Shopping Centre

The Guildhall has been used for the cover of many books about Exeter and justly so for, if we refer to the heart of Exeter, then this must surely be its pace-maker. Within its splendid interior many controversies have raged, and still do, for it serves as City Council chambers to this day – the oldest building still in such use in the country. On a day-to-day basis the Guildhall is more sombre, with droves of people reverentially pacing around inspecting the trophies and memorabilia of Exeter.

Exeter, Guildhall.

The building is one of the oldest municipal properties in England, and goes back beyond its first recorded date of about 1160. At different times various parts of the Guildhall have been used as a prison. A cellar at the front was a women's prison after 1472. Eleven years later the main hall was used temporarily for the same custodial purposes. There was another women's prison added at the back in 1521, whilst four more cells were included in 1557. The front and back prisons were known as the Fore and Back Grate respectively. Courts were also held in the Guildhall, so that frequently justice would be administered and executed under one roof. The cells were used until 1887, when Exeter received a new police station in Waterbeer Street, on a site adjacent to St Pancras Church, now part of the Guildhall Precinct; but the police station was moved to a purpose-built structure in Heavitree Road in 1960.

Through the years many colourful pageants have been witnessed at the Guildhall. The Queen has been entertained, as have many dignitaries. In contrast to this glitter, I like to think that this is a building of the people and more humble events. I particularly like the inclusions made in his book *Reminiscences of Exeter* (1878) by James Cossins: he talks of the stocks which were under the centre arch in 1830, a place of public chastisement, the sort of place some might think we could do with today!

"A passing citizen recognised a friend doing penance: 'Hello Ben, what's up with you?' 'Only a little spree last night, I'm just working out five shillings worth for two hours, I never earned so much as half-a-crown an hour before!' "

In Edwardian times the area behind the Guildhall was one of narrow streets, back-alleys (drangs) and overpopulated courts. It was an area which was tough, rough and uncompromising. It was common to hear the sound of howling from men and boys being beaten in the police station. Salt was then rubbed into the wounds. It is said that a character called Bug Whiskers would pick up cats in the street and throw them into the air as high as possible before catching them – he obviously did not like cats (and

I expect they didn't think much of him either!). The working man with a hunger attended the 'British Workman', a café where enormous helpings of everything were sold at cheap prices. The local barber used an extremely sharp 'cut-throat' razor and the fishmonger would happily whop customers across the face with a wet fish if they were cheeky. Perhaps it's just as well that the only remnants of 'those good old days' are the name Waterbeer Street and the lovely little church of St Pancras. For those who enjoy examining old maps it acts as an extremely useful marker.

Between this detached church and Queen Street pedestrians pass through the impressive columns of the former Higher Market. Above the columns it states that the rebuilt shopping centre was opened on Thursday, 11 November 1976, by HRH Princess Alexandra.

Queen Street

This is one of the straightest and flattest streets in Exeter but this wasn't always the case, because it has artificially been levelled near Central Station. This thoroughfare is generally a student conveyor belt as the daily tides ebb and flow to or from Exeter College or the University. The first road along here was Higher Market Street. The Higher Market, whose entrance fronts Queen Street, was established after 1691, when the sale of livestock in the High Street was banned.

In my youth this Higher Market, now that part of the Guildhall shopping mall marked by those classic columns at either end, was a thriving market with stone floors and bore a pervading smell of fruit and vegetables. Beside it was the multi-purpose Civic Hall, which once hosted rock concerts with bands destined to become famous – Led Zeppelin, Pink Floyd and Fleetwood Mac, to name but a few.

A statue of Queen Victoria was erected on her twenty-ninth birthday, 24 May 1848, at the High Street end of the road. However this is far from being the only artefact to be connected with Her Majesty in this, her street…

The Royal Albert Museum

This building is one geologists might appreciate: the outer walls are of purple lava from Pocombe whilst the inner walls are of red breccia from Heavitree. The limestone dressings are from Chudleigh, as they are at the Clock Tower. The window shafts are in red sandstone from Taunton, the polished pillars are of Aberdeen granite and the interior marbles (polished limestones) are from Ipplepen and Plymouth.

This edifice was obviously built in the days before Blue Circle!

The Exeter Official Publicity and Information Bureau

I am grateful to the staff of this building, which stood on the corner of Paul Street, because it was here, as a schoolboy, that I was given my first map of Dartmoor. I pinned it to the back of the toilet door and after years of quiet contemplation it proved to be the mainspring for my quest to know more about the Moor. I doubt that I would have ever written all the Dartmoor books had they not been so kind to me! It's funny how things work out.

The Clock Tower

William Miles, of Dixfield House, Exeter, was a well-known philanthropist and lover of dumb animals. Following his death his wife wished to preserve his memory in a visible way – and so the Clock Tower was erected, built of Chudleigh limestone, Corsehill and Bath stone.

Miles was especially fond of horses, and they were catered for with troughs at its base on the north and south sides. The eastern side had a fountain for travellers. Although it is a four-sided tower, internally it is circular like a lighthouse. Access, for winding and maintenance of the clock, was gained on the west side, where a door and three iron ladders led up to the four clock faces.

There has been much speculation as to the wisdom of allowing such a massive tower to remain at a junction of three busy routeways, acting as a mini-roundabout. It has been rumoured that this has been a 'Red Light' location down the years and as it is also a memorial to the reign of Queen Victoria, I doubt she would have been amused by this fact!

Exeter Prison

Nearby, the County Gaol was built between 1790 and 1794. In its early days prisoners were executed on the flat roof 'by means of a temporary apparatus'. Adjoined to these premises the House of Correction was built between 1807 and 1810 from the designs of Mr George Moneypenny who had previously designed both Leicester and Winchester gaols – coincidentally also Roman towns. Records reveal that 'its regulations are judicious, and the prisoners are employed in laborious occupations'. The Governor presided over both of these buildings. Confusingly, the date above the gateway is 1853 although parts of the 1794 building still exist. Besley's *Route Book of Devon* (1854) states that the prison had 193 cells, each 13 feet by 7 feet, and all of them had a water supply, gas light, table, stool, hammock and shelves. Food was delivered as part of room service by an ingenious method; it was conveyed 'by a carriage resting on the tramway formed by the balustrades of two opposite galleries'.

Before 1794 criminals in Exeter were held in different locations depending on the nature of their crimes. Felons were held at the Castle Yard, people in debt were held in St Thomas and both felons and debtors were held at the City and County Gaol in the South Gate, pulled down in 1819. This gave way to the new City Prison, on the same site as the Rougemont Hotel in Queen Street, which remained until it was sold in 1863.

Exeter Assizes

At this time two Assizes were held each year, one in March, the other in July. The former was the busier as more crimes were perpetrated during long winter evenings. The great influx of witnesses, interested parties and the wealthy, who turned this into something of a social occasion, meant that all the available 'rooms' in the city were taken whilst the Assizes were in progress. All the theatres were packed and people thronged the streets. Traders rubbed their hands in glee, as did other folk who benefited from the 'carnival' atmosphere.

A procession went out from the Castle to greet the judges at Heavitree, where they donned their robes before being conveyed in a state carriage belonging to the Sheriff. Crowds gathered to witness the spectacle all along the route to Exeter. When in session the crowds in the Castle Yard, or behind in Northernhay, made so much noise that courtroom proceedings could hardly be heard and it was commonplace for judges to get court attendants to try to suppress it.

On a few occasions when a jury could not agree on a verdict they were conveyed by cart into the country and unceremoniously dumped, whereupon the jury came to the unanimous opinion that they had been very badly treated! Prisoners' sentences were published in 'The Calendar of the Prisoners', a morbid document much sought after by queues of people waiting to be first to receive the details. Races to Ide, Broadclyst, Topsham, Clyst St Mary and the surrounding countryside followed, as copies were sold for good remuneration if the news was 'hot' enough.

Executions

Between 1795 and 1877 there were at least 78 executions at the County Prison. Another is recorded at the gallows in the Magdalen Road area. Several persons, like J. Bugwater, were hanged for highway robbery whilst others were executed for stealing bullocks, horses or sheep. Mr J. Haynes was hanged for rape but the majority of executions were for murder, many of these being for killing marriage partners.

When J. James and G. Champion mounted the scaffold, for their involvement in a burglary at Tiverton, a good-sized and noisy crowd were there to witness 'justice' being done. Seconds before the 'bolts' were released a blind fiddler, who had fiddled his way into earning a decent amount, suffered the indignity of having his pockets turned out. After the drama of the execution the crowd enjoyed much celebration, and the blind man's trove contributed greatly to the refreshments that the crowd enjoyed.

Charlotte Winsor was a decidedly 'lucky' lady who was sentenced to death in 1866. All the necessary preparations were made, including the construction of a gallows for her execution, a tailored coffin and a grave dug in the prison confines. Her sentence was then commuted to 'life'. However the news sheet of the day was printed before the execution and had made the assumption that it would go ahead. Her amazing story is featured in greater detail in *Murders & Mysteries in Devon* by Ann James.

Execution of Mrs. Winsor

At Exeter,

For the barbarous murder of Mary Jane Harris's Child

Thousands of people massed in Exeter to gaze at the executions. The fields where Exeter Central railway station was later sited were packed, as were the slopes of Northernhay. At noon the High Street would be deserted and the hangman was ready to perform. If it was a murderer, his corpse was taken to the hospital for dissection; for other crimes the corpses were taken to the 'dead house' where bodies could be inspected. After 1869 all executions were within the prison confines.

John ('Babbacombe') Lee

A most amazing and astonishing story surrounds this man, referred to as 'the man they could not hang'. At the age of 15 John Lee took up a junior position with Miss Emma Keyse at her home in Babbacombe (it has since been pulled down and the public conveniences at Babbacombe Beach are located on the spot). He went to sea but was invalided out of the Navy with pneumonia. After a short spell with the Great Western Railway he went to work for Colonel Brownlow in Torquay. When the Brownlows were abroad he pawned some of their silver, for which he served six months hard labour at Exeter Prison. Upon his release John, now 20 (1884), was offered his old job back with Miss Keyse. He settled down and started courting a local girl, the sound of wedding bells in the air. Shortly after Miss Keyse had dropped his pay from 2/6d (12½p) to 2s (10p) her charred corpse was found with a broken neck and cut throat. Lee was the obvious suspect as the only man in the house. He was committed for trial in December and faced the charge in early February 1885. Miss Keyse had been famous and popular in Torquay; Queen Victoria had been known to visit her mother and she was loved by many influential people. It is believed that this was one of the primary causes why John Lee's defence counsel seemed to offer little resistance to venomous prosecution. Lee sat surprisingly calm and passive through the entire trial. Even when the judge donned his black cap to pronounce the death sentence Lee appeared unruffled. When the judge had finished Lee rose to his feet and said, "The reason, My Lord, why I am so calm and collected is because I trust the Lord, and he knows I am innocent."

The execution date was set for 23 February but the day before that he told his warders that he had dreamed the scaffold would fail to work on three occasions. This was duly recorded in the Governor's log. Also in his dream he envisaged taking a different route to the scaffold, which perplexed him a little. Ironically the procession took the very route of which he had dreamed.

The Reverend Pitkin read the service for the Burial of the Dead and James Berry, the famous executioner, was ready. On the stroke of 8 a.m. the vicar reached the last words and Berry pulled the lever. The whole structure shuddered but the trap door remained closed. A few minutes of frenzied activity followed. Lee kept his white cap on, his legs still bound; the rope still around his neck. Nothing was wrong with the doors and the chaplain read again the last few words of the service. Berry pulled the lever again but the trap doors remained firm.

Lee was led away whilst adjustments were made and tests performed – the scaffold was in perfect working order. At 8.20 a.m. the executioner was ready again. A length of rope eight feet long was draped around Lee's neck. The chaplain uttered the last lines again but still the trap door did not open. Lee was untied, his white cap and the rope were removed. Deathly white, he was taken back to the condemned cell. The Sheriff sought advice from higher authorities which resulted in the sentence being commuted to life.

John Lee went to Portland Prison to serve his sentence feeling that he had not cheated death but had received a fairer supernatural judicial decision. One newspaper had jumped the gun and had reported that the execution had taken place as planned. Some journalists had witnessed this amazing spectacle, having a good viewpoint arranged by the Governor of the prison.

Lee survived his sentence, married a girl called Jessie Bulleid and fathered two daughters. Some say he went to Australia, others plump for the United States. He was seen in London in late 1911 and his wife is known to have claimed parish relief for herself and the children the following year.

In 1917 a silent movie was made about Lee's life story, and in Cardiff 50,000 people flocked to see it in one week. Many of Lee's relations, from his native Abbotskerswell, turned up to see the film at Newton Abbot. Television documentaries have been made and Fairport Convention, a folk-rock group, did an LP about John (Babbacombe) Lee's life story.

At a funeral in Torquay in the 1920s, a mourner clearly stated that buried with the coffin was the secret of Emma Keyse's killer ... So, was John Lee a very lucky man to survive the gallows, or was it the Divine Hand of Fate intervening on his behalf?

The full and compelling story is another told in the marvellous *Murders & Mysteries in Devon* by Ann James.

The Underground Passages

Although Exeter is not blessed by any natural caves, through a lack of limestone, it still manages to afford would-be subterranean explorers an underground experience, but in man-made surroundings.

To date these passages positively is difficult as additions and alterations have caused historians plenty of headscratching. Most seem to settle for the first recorded date of any mention, which was 1226. However, some like to think that parts of the passages are Roman.

One theory put forward is that the conduit approached the Roman Baths, now beneath the paved area in front of the Cathedral. It was thought that the water was piped under the present Cathedral Yard and possibly beneath this fires were lit to provide a hot water supply to these baths. History seems to suggest that these conduits were constructed to take the waters from the powerful springs which supplied the Long Brook but were sited beyond the City Wall. Undoubtedly the passages were cleverly engineered on the gentlest of gradients. This allowed the waters to reach the Cathedral area without erosion of the soft red rocks in the passages. Their shape was also designed to facilitate the flow. However, the waters suffered from contamination so they were put into lead pipes during the fourteenth century. Along the passage will be seen 'dipping' or 'pot water' holes which were used by houses above the passages, but these lost the supply when it became piped.

A guided tour, not to be missed by visitors or locals, passes beneath the top of the High Street, part of Princesshay and Longbrook Street. The passages were rendered fit for opening to the public after the last war but although the network extends for several miles beneath the city, difficulties such as cave-ins, caused by bomb damage, have reduced the amount of passages which can be safely and easily followed. On a hot day the cool damp atmosphere, below ground, will make a stark contrast but having acclimatised, the visitor will be taken along passages of varying heights and widths, some bricked, others rough hewn. The passages attract a greater number of visitors on wet days when tourists flock into the City from the coast.

Georgian Southernhay

This is a green and pleasant corner of Exeter, revealing a striking floral beauty overlooked by fine Georgian buildings. These town houses, once the properties of traders, merchants and dignitaries, have seen a change in fortunes and functions; now they are insurance offices, estate agents, solicitors, dentists and so on. Within a short distance of the Roman Wall are many examples of other Georgian terraces which include those of Barnfield, Colleton and Dix's Field. Alas, many others were destroyed in the blitz, the most notable being Bedford Circus, now Bedford Street.

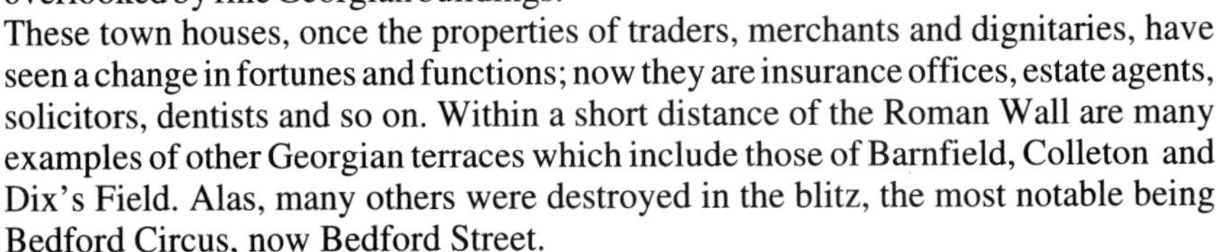

Georgian Exeter was the sixth largest city in England and it enjoyed much trade with the continent, Holland in particular. Many of Exeter's merchants made fortunes from the wine trade with Spain and Portugal but it was the wool trade that was the main industry which sustained a wealthy style of living for its merchants. As a measure of relative importance, Exeter boasted the third newspaper to be launched outside London and by 1714 Exeter had the *Mercury*, the *Post Boy* and the *Post Man* to further illustrate its status.

Until 1823 a horse fair was held between Dix's Field and Barnfield, on what is now the upper green. Menageries, booths and shows were also held there before being removed to Bonhay.

A small footbridge links the breached ramparts of the Roman Wall and includes the words 'Burnet Patch, Mayor Exeter, 1814'. The bridge enabled the Muraltie Walk along the top of the wall to be made. This went around the entire perimeter of the wall, the walk having been inaugurated during the fourteenth century. Every Michaelmas Day the new Mayor and the City Corporation did this walk to inspect any damage.

Southernhay was a refuge for bishops escaping from the plague-ridden City. They reached the green fields by way of Lollard's Tower, a bastion built in 1623.

A long-forgotten 'Public Baths', supplied by the City Water Works from Bonhay Road, existed where Broadwalk House now stands. On offer were 'cold, hot, plunge, shower, vapour, medicated and fumigated baths'.

The White Hart

The hotel, in South Street, has a deceptively narrow frontage veiling a building with many bars, courtyards and 60 bedrooms – Exeter's answer to Dr Who's Tardis. It is strange that people will go on guided tours of museums, large houses, cathedrals and churches but rarely consider the wealth of fascinating relics in places like the White Hart. Thankfully that wonderful historian, the late W. G. Hoskins, had the foresight to film many scenes there for a series for the BBC in 1975.

The White Hart (the favourite badge of Richard III) is sited beside the former South Gate, which for several centuries was the main routeway into and out of the City. It was handily located to serve the needs of travellers, and teams of carriers and their files of pack-horses used the inn. The courtyard, which later also stabled horse-drawn conveyances, is now a car park. Only a little imagination is required to picture the scenes of yesteryear.

It is believed that William Wynard used it as his private residence in the fifteenth century and in his time it later became the Blue Boar Inn. Wynard, a benevolent fellow, had endowed his new hospital with many buildings including this one. 'Wynards', in Magdalen Street, still serves the community, not as a leper hospital, but its many good organisations try to help people in various ways.

Less fortunate though was a carpenter who was called to the White Hart to repair a well. At the bottom he suddenly collapsed and died. A second person followed only to succumb to the same fate. Bravely, or perhaps foolishly, a third person tried to aid the others. He almost perished but lived to explain that there was an evil stench in the pit, presumably carbonic acid gas. I think this proves you should treat the sick and leave the well alone!

Many famous visitors have stayed at the hotel, including the *Monty Python's Flying Circus* team who filmed sketches at Cowick Street and Higher King's Avenue in Exeter. A visitors' book for the famous has just been started. Steve Davis, the former world snooker champion, was one of the first to sign it.

Another White Hart existed in Longbrook Street during the last century. Its celebrated host was one Jenkin Williams, a Welshman, whose main claim to notoriety was his pipe-smoking exploits; he managed to be on his tenth pipe of the day by 10 o'clock each morning.

The West Quarter

In that area between South Street, Fore Street and the river, there used to be a twilight area known as the West Quarter. Several generations ago Tommy Linscott, and Jo Brooking (by the Guildhall), were pawnbrokers, 'trading' in a part of the City notorious for its squalor, poverty and toughness. The West Quarter was a precinct of the City where policemen patrolled in pairs, and young children learned to fend for themselves from an early age. Some wives pawned their husbands' Sunday-best clothes on a Monday only to redeem them later in the week. Times were so hard that any item of value would eventually find its way to either Linscott or Brooking, who took their cut at both ends of any transaction. The system apparently worked well, with a pawn-broker's representative patrolling the streets every Monday calling out, “Any pawn”. Items clearly labelled with the owner’s mark were whisked away. Although it was possible to borrow hard cash, the rate of repayment to money-lenders was prohibitive and to pawn was viewed as an acceptable alternative.

The local morgue was in Coombe Street and it’s macabre to discover that for a short time at least it became Bosuns night-club. There was also a Mission Hall which served a ‘farthing breakfast’ (there were 960 farthings in a pound!) which comprised a small sliced loaf with margarine and jam, and as much cocoa as could be consumed. The feast was usually well attended.

People lived in overcrowded accommodation and probably worked in one of the many factories close by. There were the cattlemarket and slaughterhouse in Bonhay Road; J. L. Thomas, which made soap and candles amidst an unholy stench; Tremletts, a rat-infested tannery; Bradbeers, a brush factory; and various flour mills. Work was never against the grain of people from this area, who often toiled hard and long for little reward or social betterment.

Statistics clearly show that the people of the West Quarter endured the worst living conditions of any district in south-west England, which must surely have accounted for their low life expectancy and vulnerability to contagious illnesses. A combination of all these factors resulted in the local authority setting up a programme to clear the worst of the slums.

In 1928 about 580 insanitary homes were demolished and nearly 2,500 people were rehoused on a large council estate at Burnthouse Lane, then on the outskirts of Exeter. A great many unskilled and poorly educated people were uprooted and rehoused. They felt that they were so far from Exeter and civilisation that they took to naming the new estate ‘Siberia’. Contemporary records show that although their immediate housing conditions vastly improved, their health record didn’t. Within a few years the Burnthouse Lane estate had become the most densely populated area, per room, of any part of south-west England.

However, the West Quarter did have the distinction of having the first fish and chip shop in the City, in Guinea Street, opened by Mr John Preston, a Bristolian.

Much rebuilding has taken place in the area as it has been severely altered. The old pattern of streets is identifiable, as are pockets of old buildings, but the slums have gone and also, many years later, the taller tenements. This picture shows Follett Buildings. The local school was fondly nicknamed 'Rack Street Naval College', probably because many of its boy pupils became sailors on leaving school, at an early age, possibly to escape to what they saw as a better life. A great deal of imagination is necessary to envisage, today, the scenes of abject poverty and urban blight found here. Much new housing, of a high standard of amenity, stands where insanitary and vastly overcrowded slum dwellings once existed.

Fore Street

There is no other street in Exeter quite like it. It is possible to buy anything from Nazi war souvenirs to naughty knick-knacks, from boomerangs to banjos, from G-strings to G-strings! The diverse and amazing range of shops and places of refreshment has created a shopping and socialising environment which has been referred to, by some, as Exeter's answer to London's Carnaby Street.

Evidence that larger chain stores predicted the decline of trade in Fore Street can be seen at David's furniture shop, where Bobby's (now Debenhams), an important store, moved to a site higher in the town in 1964. The word 'Bobby's' is still etched in the shop floor entrance. Anyone who looks up at the upper storeys of buildings in the street will notice the great variety in the heights and designs of them, many Georgian in age. The upper part of the former Wheaton's building, at 143 Fore Street, where Charles Dickens once stayed, reveals an attractive frontage missed by the masses who mosey past. I must confess that I never noticed even though I worked there through the entire summer of 1966! At that time there were a number of long-established businesses which presented a permanant face to this street but one by one they have gone. Exonians may recall the likes of Lesbert (photogra-

pher), Walter Otton (ironmonger), Norton (cycle shop), Knapman (building merchants/decorators), Hurved (grocer), Forte's Café, the Silver Grill restaurant, Woodhouse and Hampshire (both furniture stores) and Blake's (surgical stores) and a host of others, in a street which now sees a more rapid turnover in businesses. But some have stayed to ride the tides of change and Thomas Moore (clothing) and Bill Greenalgh (music shop) provide some stability and continuity.

Fore Street, despite its aging buildings, many of which have been the victim of major blazes, has plenty to interest the explorer bored by the predictable line-up found in most modern shopping centres. The historian will also find Tuckers Hall, a building associated with Exeter's past lucrative wool trade, steeped in history. Opening times are displayed outside.

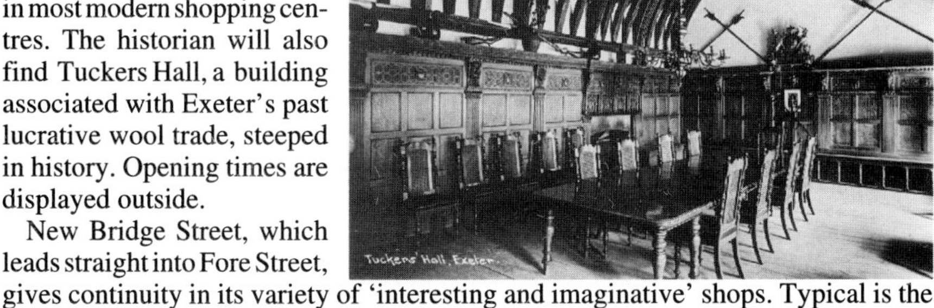

New Bridge Street, which leads straight into Fore Street, gives continuity in its variety of 'interesting and imaginative' shops. Typical is the long-established Gordon Truman which sells apparel much of which one would find impossible to buy in any chain shop. Bikers, line dancers, cowboys and others who need 'specialist wear' are catered for. The brilliant and colourful mural on the gable end of the end building, is the work of the 'elusive' Andrew Stacey, an artist who has much of his work in evidence around the city, including other fine murals in Holloway Street and Chute Street.

Bartholomew Street

The Exeter Civic Society made a comprehensive study of the Bartholomew Street area and in 1977 produced a report called 'Restoration or Demolition?' In it they studied the decaying nature of the area and accounted for this trend. Once these problems were identified they put forward some practical suggestions to enable the area to regain its pride, usefulness and identity.

In the past a Celtic (British) village existed there. Their descendants continued on through Saxon times, when it was known as 'Britayne' – Tozer's map of 1792 refers to it as 'Little Britain'.

From 1691 the area was dominated by cattle and pigs at a market removed to there from the High Street; this continued for 125 years.

Most of the houses in the area were built between 1800 and 1840 but in recent years have shown signs of decay. Initially these were occupied by well-to-do people but as time progressed the area changed its character. One of the houses, beside the original St Wilfred's School, has a painted exterior. At shoulder level the paintwork was smoothed down to the thinnest coating imaginable when a resident tramp spent many hours scratching himself against the door!

The emphasis on rehabilitation and restoration is closely allied to the development of a community atmosphere again. The Exeter Civic Society should be congratulated for their work in this respect.

The Catacombs – Bartholomew Street

These were built on the side of the Longbrook valley, in 1837, as burial vaults. The Jews and non-believers were laid to rest on the Iron Bridge side of the entrance whilst the Christians were interred on the Snayle Tower side. The Egyptian-styled catacombs' builders took advantage of the wall incorporating the tumuli. Victorian speculators must have worked on a theory which said that even though you couldn't take your money with you when you died, at least you could go in as much comfort as possible. These spacious, built-for-profit, vaults consisted of a long central passage with vaulted recesses opening off on each side. These were going to be honeycombed but only one was completed this way.

Coffins were lowered from street level into the vaults through a roof. These were then sealed by a grave stone stating the appropriate details of the deceased. Only 15 people were ever interred there, the last in 1883.

The speculator who built the vaults lost a lot of money on the venture and the situation was so 'grave' that the City took them over. They partitioned off part of them to produce a building which served as a mortuary.

I always get the impression that had 'Hammer House of Horror' films been made in this part of the world then this would have been the perfect location. Check with the local Tourist Information Centre for times of opening.

The Iron Bridge

A look across the deep natural depression of the Longbrook valley will reveal the six-arched viaduct simply called the Iron Bridge. It was cast in South Wales and bears the inscription 'Russell and Brown's Iron Works 1834'. Its arches each have a span of 40 feet, and its length is about 800 feet. The 'Improvement Commissioners', who funded the construction of the bridge, had even considered a suspension bridge across this natural dip.

At the city end there is a plaque which records the former position of the North Gate, which was removed in 1794. Beside this is a tall pole bears a weather-griffin, a strange creature, half-cockerel and half-dragon and most unlike a typical weather vane. It is ornamented with gold foil, and was re-erected by the Exeter Civic Society.

Paul Street

In a city which has developed in a piecemeal fashion there have been some horrendous examples of streets with real character being made almost soulless and Paul Street is about the best example. I cannot begin to imagine what the late, great Walter Daw (a school was named in his honour) would have to say about this street's changes. He was born here in Edwardian times when the street was full of businesses, and although it was another 'no nonsense' place to grow up, at least it was alive with workaday people going about their daily tasks. Having seen his splendid 'slide show' of how it used to be, the changes which have occurred in this part of the city have been dramatic. From 1902 the Council started buying up shops on the north-west side of the street. Their intention was to widen the street and to create a new public library and civic centre on the junction with Queen Street, where the Museum Hotel had stood. The first tourist information centre later occupied the site for a number of years. By 1922 most of the properties were derelict and in a dangerous state; by 1928 they had all gone! However, the new civic buildings never materialised. This picture shows Richard Mears who ran his business at 7 Paul Street. He moved out to Locarno Road where he lived until his death in 1953.

Throughout my childhood, in the 1950s and '60s, the street still had its small shops, pubs and cafés on its south-east side, with the bus and coach station opposite.

However the wind of change has blown, yet again, through this functional, but featureless thoroughfare with the building of the adjacent 'Golden Heart' or Guildhall Centre and the multi-storey car parks. The end result is a gloomy street of towering walls, of queueing traffic, a visual disaster which gives a very poor impression to those arriving in the city for the first time.

North Street

If you compare these small pictures you will see that the same sort of changes which blighted Paul Street, just around the corner, have been evident in North Street as well. Older Exonians will have their own memories but my recollections hark back to the times when I was a pupil, in the 1960s, at Episcopal School, having to walk down and up North Street twice a day: pasties from Boon's, fish and chips from Forte's; second-hand 'anything' from Bland Brothers; an occasional meal in the Austrian Café or Watty's on the opposite side of the street; my classmate, Bob Gilbert, whose dad ran the Elephant Inn; the Gaumont Cinema and 'Saturday morning pictures'; Brocks, Mansfield, Garton & King, Troulan, Chudley's, and so it went on, mostly names no longer there. Cornish's were on the top corner of the street, with their slow moving lift, the first one installed in Exeter. They kitted out many Exeter schoolchildren with uniforms and also provided me with my first pair of long trousers and this on my thirteenth birthday! How times, and waistlines, have changed in the 'Lost City of Exeter'!

Along the Waterfront

The River Exe starts in Somerset, high on Exmoor, bubbling up in the middle of a moorland morass, a wilderness place if ever there was one. It flows from its infant beginnings to accept the waters of a great number of smaller streams and rivers as it flows ever southwards carving out an impressive and beautiful valley. By the time it reaches the relative lowlands of Exeter it is a major feature of the landscape. It is the principal reason why a settlement of importance exists at Exeter, because once upon a time, given a low tide, the river could be forded here. Generally at such points settlements normally developed but the Exe had more to offer than just a crossing place. The river was so well oxygenated by its turbulent and unpolluted waters, it carried an enormous population of game fish such as trout and salmon, a useful source of food, a natural form of 'take away'! 'Exe', from which Exeter is derived, literally means 'a river abounding in fish'. However, over the centuries the river has been constrained and its course greatly altered. Now it is only about a third as wide as it was a thousand years ago, but three times as deep, constrained in man-made banks.

The city's waterfront is an area to be explored on foot or by bicycle. The mile-long section from the weirs in Bonhay Road to Trew's Weir in St Leonard's reveals a lot about Exeter's past. Although the noise of an urban environment is often close at hand, it is possible, for most of the way, to escape from the intrusion of wheeled traffic – discounting, of course, prams, pushchairs, wheelchairs, skateboards, rollerskates and bikes!

Swimming in the Exe – A Dip into History!

The waters of the Exe have been ponded by the Head and Blackaller Weirs. Above them there once existed a public swimming pool in the river. Access to the riverside changing huts was close to where the railway line from St David's Station to Central Station crosses Bonhay Road. For several decades an attendant and life guard were frequently on duty to patrol the roped-off pool, where many people swam in warm weather. A rowing boat was used to patrol the perimeter of the pool. The personnel who ran the 'Head Weir Bathing Place' had to be vigilant. One of the earliest 'bathing

constables', and later 'bathing superintendent', was Frank Shooter, a professional swimmer and a man of great note who was at Head Weir in the latter years of the nineteenth century, for a total of some 37 years. He is credited with having rescued about 200 people who got into difficulties. One of his main interests outside of water activities was boxing, and in this field he was more than competent. His 'cubicle' walls at Head Weir were covered with photos of the top boxers of his day. However, it was in the water that he was supreme. One of his party pieces was to dive into the Exe and surface smoking a lit cigar, much to the amazement and delight of onlookers. He passed away in 1917. John Bates ('Tich') and Frank Hutchings ('Ducko') were later in charge, in the early decades of the twentieth century.

For those folk who lived in houses without running water, this was about their only opportunity to wash so they took soap with them! Swimmers were segregated; most sessions were for 'men only' with women only able to enjoy a dip on a few occasions each week. A warning was issued to all not to stray over to the far bank as the weeds were dangerous; nesting swans were another menace. The pool was open from 1 May, each season, and it was thought quite 'brave' to manage a dip on the first day. No signs or remnants of this 'pool' exist today as the line of bathing huts was removed many years ago.

The opening of an indoor swimming pool at King Street (a former narrow opening opposite St Stephen's Bow in the High Street) meant that the luxury of all-year-round bathing could be enjoyed. The former King Street baths were used to give returning soldiers of many nationalities a cleansing dip after the D-Day operations; after this they were accommodated at the adjacent YMCA. The current swimming bath in Heavitree Road dates back to the late 1930s but has been refurbished in an Egyptian style and is now aptly named 'Pyramids'.

Exe Island

Before the tenth century this was a watery wilderness of reed beds and mud flats. However, its level site beneath the city wall attracted the attention of early speculators. In 1194 Nicholas Gervase obtained a grant from Robert de Courtenay to build a mill. The Courtenays (later Earls of Devon) held the land between the wall and the river known as Exe Island (*Insula Ex* on early documents). What may have appeared to have been a wasteland of marsh and mire became a most productive area for the Courtenays as they capitalised on its potential. Drains or leats were networked across it and some levees raised the land sufficiently to dry it out. Leats were used from the twelfth century to power water mills. From that time on, Exe Island was an early industrial area with many mills, powered by between 20 and 30 waterwheels. It remained in their possession until the family lost favour in 1538; in 1550 King Edward VI gave this land to the City.

Today most people cross 'Exe Island' without a passing thought for what it was like in the past. In the 1960s, like its lowland counterpart of St Thomas, beyond the river, it suffered from floods, a reminder of times past.

For a long while Exeter's drinking water was extracted from the River Exe at a pumping station located where Exe Street meets Bonhay Road. The bridge at that point is called Engine Bridge after the device which pumped the water up to the town.

Until 1939 Exeter's cattle market was at Bonhay Road – the aerial photograph shows the enclosures. On one occasion a bull escaped, charged up a fire escape of an

adjacent building, and ended up in the bathroom in a real lather! In trying to escape though, the poor beast injured itself and was put down.

It is said that the nearby slaughterhouse discharged so much blood that when the leats were in full flow they ran red. It was common for manhole covers to be pushed up and for the bloody pools to inundate buildings. During the first half of the century, when refrigeration and other cryogenic methods of preserving foodstuffs had not been invented, butchers in Exeter looked to the Ice Works in Bonhay Road to solve their problems. Ice could be bought in blocks or food stored for a fee. For many years the Army stored thousands of tins of corned beef, left over from the First World War, at the Ice Works and ran up a massive bill. Like so many of Exeter's buildings, it eventually burned down. The markets, Ice Works, slaughterhouse, some of the pubs and the original police station have also all gone.

Parkin's and the Eagle Foundry were two foundries which competed with each other. Francis Parkin's firm, which began in 1847, is still around, having expanded greatly from humble beginnings, and has now relocated to the Marsh Barton estate.

When I was a schoolboy we did a study of the surroundings of this area. The visit to the former paper mill at Head Weir was a memorable one and I can vividly recall that it was a building full of ladders, walkways, draughty spaces, noise and atmosphere. The mill closed in 1967 and a large part of it was demolished in 1982. Part of it is now the beautifully located 'Mill on the Exe' pub.

The leats of Exe Island have largely been filled in but one still flows shyly around the back of Tudor Street, crosses the inner bypass, passes along to the Custom House and into the Exe.

Exe Bridges

Much has been written about this, a focal point of traffic, where routes converge to cross the river, not the best place to be in the rush-hour. In the past, as we have seen, the river was far wider than it is now, and the earlier bridge had to be much longer than the present ones to allow for this. At low tide it was possible to wade across, the nearest point to the sea that this could be done. However, many a poor person lost his life attempting this. The first many-arched stone bridge was completed about 1238. It carried a lot of traffic of the pedestrian and packhorse kind before being completely overhauled in 1449. And it was the City's rapid growth again, in Georgian times, which resulted in the need for a wider structure. A three-arched bridge was started in 1770 but floods caused extensive damage, its architect was dismissed and a new one employed. When this 'new' Exe bridge was completed, the first vehicles to cross were those of a funeral cortège.

Another Exe Bridge opened in 1905 as a result of the further increase in traffic, notably horse-drawn trams. Its old lamp standards can now be seen setting off Butts Ferry at Exeter Quay complete with striking coat of arms. This bridge was demolished in 1974. The two present structures that replaced it are basic but functional and enable a great volume of traffic to pass over them, but at peak times long jams still form on the approach roads.

Shilhay

Shilhay is an area once again inhabited, by folk housed in a 'village-style' community. Its design has won accolades from some but brickbats from others who live there, close to the nightclub heartland of the city. Its existence was at the expense of a proposed leisure centre which, at the time, caused a storm of controversy. There are many in Exeter who feel that all, or most, of the city's leisure and recreational facilities could have been, with imagination and flair, located on the Shilhay. Such a major leisure complex, using the waterfront's potential, would undoubtedly have nipped some of the area's present problems in the bud...

However, the Shilhay residential scheme has been thoughtfully named. The various 'courts' have been christened after terms connected with the wool trade, carried on at the site, hitting a peak between 1670 and 1720 when about 300,000 cloths a year were being exported from Exeter. Indicative of this past trade are the names of Carders, Dyers, Serge, Fullers, Shearman, Teazle and Weavers Courts.

Tuckers and Fullers removed the grease from the wool. An inspection of the local telephone directory reveals a great number of Tuckers and Fullers locally, whose names, presumably, have been handed down as a result of these activities. Carders combed the wool with a hooked instrument. *Carduus* is a type of thistle from which carders took their name, whilst the teazle was initially used to bring up the nap of the wool. This plant is often found in the coat of arms of wool towns, Ashburton being a good local example. Serge was hand-woven worsted, usually with a twill weave.

A name unconnected with that trade is Gabriel Court, taken from the former Gabriel's Wharf which existed on 'Coney Lake' ('coney' means 'rabbit' and 'lake' means 'stream'), one of the many leats which flowed through the Bonhay and Shilhay areas. The name Shilhay can be easily interpreted, 'hay' meaning an enclosed or fenced area and 'shil' a ledge or shelf. The name is common in the Dartmoor area with Shilston Tor also warranting a shelf-like description. The Shilhay in its heyday was a shelf of land just above the river level. No doubt in pre-Roman times when the Exe was free from the constraints of the many weirs which repel the tides, the Shilhay was constantly under water. For this reason the Shilhay and Bonhay areas were not sited until the land was drained by the building of leats in the medieval period.

Opposite the new housing scheme is a pub which has witnessed all the modern upheaval, The Bishop Blaize. It is unlikely that many will appreciate the link between the inn's name and the history of its immediate surroundings. Bishop Blaize was the Patron Saint of the wool trade, which is apt in the circumstances. This picture is how it looked during the floods of 1960.

Beside the Bishop Blaize used to be W. G. Shears, corn merchant. The Shears family occupied these premises for many years, and once used the site as a corn and grist mill. Their former property included 'Cricklepit Mill' beneath the city wall. This ancient name was reused in the naming of the modern pedestrian suspension bridge spanning the Exe near the Quay.

In Cricklepit Lane, legend has it that Matthew the Miller produced his fine flour in a systematic way. Indeed he had such a regular routine that all the folk nearby knew what time it was by watching Matthew at work. When he died the local populace was at a loss as to what the time of day was and in his honour collected sufficient funds to erect an elaborate clock on St Mary Steps Church near the West Gate. Sat beside him were his two 'sons'. Other historic documents, however, support different theories as to the placement of the clock named 'Matthew the Miller'. Many believe that the main figure is Henry VIII with two soldiers or javelin men in attendance.

On the page opposite is a sequence of photos showing the 'house that moved' being moved in December 1961 to its new home beside the West Gate. This fine Tudor building was saved from demolition, having originally stood in the path of a new road built to improve the traffic flow near Exe Bridge.

The riverside area has seen more change than it could have ever imagined. Firms like J. L. Thomas which made soap and candles, and Tremletts the hide and skin tannery, gave the area a seedy, unpleasant atmosphere; the latter encouraged a vast population of rats.

The decaying nature of this twilight zone meant that for years tramps and vagabonds would visit the 'doss house' at Gabriel's Wharf. Often those who could not find four-walled accommodation turned to the one Roman wall. In those 'pre-*Big Issue*' days, when the Simon Community's Gabriel's Wharf hostel was full, those who couldn't get in slept rough, through starry, starry nights to wake on crisp but penetrating frosty morns in this lane. On such occasions they could be seen bedded down with all their worldly goods tied up in bundles as pillows and softeners.

Closer to the Quay a group of bonded warehouses are now nightspots, converted in the 1960s. Initially this was seen as a good location, being well away from populated areas where noise levels were not so critical. Unfortunately, ever since the Shilhay residential scheme was built there has been, at times, conflict between rowdy, drunken 'nightclubbers' and irate residents, which is hardly surprising given the closeness of the two factions.

1 *2*

3 *4*

The Quay

Man has cunningly veiled the natural landscape which once existed in this section of the River Exe. From Larkbeare, a quarter mile to the south, to St David's, a mile to the north, there was an unbroken line of steep hills and cliffs flanking the eastern margin of the Exe. On the western side of the Exe an extensive swamp, often underwater, stretched away south-westwards beyond St Thomas to the foot of the nearby hills. The natural red sandstone shelf, where the Quay is sited, was the best location to unload cargoes.

Now that trade has ceased, the Quay and its warehouses have undertaken a new lease of life as an area which attracts tourists. On a fine day the atmosphere is of relaxation and recreation. Fishing, walking, cycling, canoeing, boating and sightseeing are all prevalent activities. The Exe sees many spectacles between Trew's Weir and Head Weir with regattas, power boating, crazy-craft races and festivals taking place.

The Quay was developed into the area we recognise today as long ago as 1564, at the same time when John Trew was engineering the first Exeter Canal. Down the years it has been a working area, with boats congesting the waterfront so tightly that they had to moor two or three deep. This vast amount of trade suddenly diminished when the railway reached Exeter in 1844. By the turn of the century visiting vessels could choose their berth, St Leonard's Quay had gone and most cargoes were hauled to and from coastal ports by rail. There was even some talk of routing a line along the eastern bank to the Quay but the engineering difficulties and debatable economic viability meant that the planners had to think along new lines to serve the waterfront. The result of their rethinking can be seen in the route of the former branch line which led to the Canal Basin.

The warehouses along the Quay had progressively less goods pass through them as sugar and timber moved into vessels much too big to reach Exeter. To utilise the vacated spaces of the warehouse cellars, a variety of tradesmen and merchants moved in to occupy the premises. In the 1950s and '60s a lot of small businesses established themselves, several of them thriving in the most unusual of situations. However, rules and regulations, governing such essential aspects as safety at work and hygiene, were introduced and many small businesses ceased operating along this waterfront. The sheds closer to Colleton Hill have given away to luxury flats overlooking the river. Having grown up in St Leonard's, and having spent many hours fishing along these river banks, I remember the hub of activity along here. In 1965 Herbie Plain could be seen here, at number 10 The Quay, working on his beloved motorbikes. Mr Sanford (whose son, Tony, an old schoolmate and friend of mine, was tragically killed in a speedway accident in 1981), was always a friendly face going about his work as a firewood merchant at number 21. In the sheds I remember James Bee, the coal merchant and, of course, there was the HQ for 19th Exeter group of Sea Scouts who often splashed about in the river. Where the Interpretation Centre gives tourists a taste of Exeter's history there used to be a DIY store – despite the many years since its passing, I can still smell the sawdust!

Bollards to the Left of me, Cannons to the Right!

When growing up I first noticed one of the bollards on the Quay when I inadvertently rode into it on my bicycle – I still bear the scar on my knee as a lasting memory. Little did I know (or care then) the history behind this piece of street furniture, which was originally a Russian cannon, one of a number to find itself in Exeter. Two of them were lovingly restored in the 1980s and are now displayed on well-crafted gun carriages strategically positioned in front of the Custom House.

This, however is not the full story and I am grateful to J. Flower for this more detailed account of the situation. *"In 1815 after the Battle of Waterloo, a committee was set up in Wellington to erect a memorial to commemorate the achievements of the Duke of Wellington. On 20 October 1817, the foundation stone was laid by Lord Somerville. At a subsequent dinner in the White Hart Inn at Wellington following the ceremony, it was announced that the Prince Regent had agreed to present four cannons to be placed at the foot of the monument, such cannon having been used at the Battle of Waterloo.*

Between October 1817 and 1819 the cannons duly arrived at Exeter Quay by sea; sixteen in number and not four, comprising fifteen iron and one bronze, a total weight of 40 tons 5 cwt.

Following enquiries made by letter to the Chief Inspector of Artillery at Woolwich at that time it was ascertained that the fifteen iron cannons were made in Scotland by the Carron Company in 1789 for the Empress of Russia, Catherine the Great. The cannons were shipped from Grangemouth on 29 June 1789 to Archangel in Russia. These cannons became obsolete in 1800 and were still in Russia at the time of the Battle of Waterloo.

The original consignment of cannons to Russia, of which the fifteen that arrived subsequently in Exeter formed part, were used for arming the Russian fleet. A small consignment of the cannons were returned to England following the defeat of Napoleon as being surplus to requirements. Out of this consignment fifteen guns were sent to Exeter. Following their arrival the Memorial Committee found out that these guns were in fact naval guns and had not been used at the Battle of Waterloo. The City Council were asked by Lord Somerville if the guns could be stored on Exeter Quay until a decision was made, which was agreed on 14 October 1819. On 21 January 1824 the City Council informed the Memorial Committee that unless they received a decision, and the cannons removed in three months, the Council would sell them to defray costs. In August 1824 the bronze cannon was sold for £54. Four of the fifteen iron cannons were sunk in the Quay for bollards and the remainder buried.

The Wellington Monument was eventually completed in 1854, after many delays.

In December 1890 Mr E. Jeboult, Taunton historian, wrote to Exeter City Council asking for the four cannons being used as bollards to be sent to the Wellington Monument. The Council did not excavate the cannons and did not send them to Wellington as they had no connection with the Battle of Waterloo.

A few years after this request the eleven buried cannons were dug up and found to be in good condition, and subsequently four were sent to the Wellington Monument and mounted on wooden carriages. The remaining seven were mounted in Bull Meadow Park. During the 1939/45 War, the four cannons mounted at Wellington were removed for scrap for the war effort, and the cannons in Bull Meadow Park met the same fate. The remaining four cannons used as bollards on the Quay remained the only ones to survive from the original consignment ... These cannons are 32 pounders weighing three tons each and similar to those used at the Battle of Trafalgar."

One of the cannons was presented to the Wellington Monument Committee, arriving there more than 160 years after setting off from Russia.

The Onedin Line

If you are ever in the Prospect Inn, have a look at some of the pictures which grace the walls for they show 'stills' from the filming of a series which ran and ran and was shown around the world. *The Onedin Line* filmed many scenes on Exeter Quay as, for the story, it played the part of mid-Victorian Liverpool, a role it shared with Dartmouth's Bayard's Cove. Liverpool was unsuitable for filming so these two Devon ports were seen as ideal for the two series filmed in 1971 and 1976. Exeter was particularly good for filming because, unlike the Dart, it wasn't tidal, so shots showing the water could be taken at any time making continuity much easier.

More can read about the filming of this and many other films and tv programmes in another of my books called *Made in Devon*. It is surprising that Exeter Quay was not renamed 'Onedin Quay' because this would have drawn millions of visitors to it. One only has to look at 'Summer Wine' or 'Emmerdale' country to see the power of television.

Butts Ferry

The small ferry which plies its way from 'Shooting Marsh Stile', now just a name, to the Quay has done so since at least 1750, despite threats to its existence, and even though there have been many different ferrymen and families working it! It is one of the only ferries in Europe which is manipulated by hand. The wire, upon which it runs, has caused some nasty accidents as unsuspecting river mariners have failed to spot it in time.

One ferryman, a typical old river-salt, who was fond of enjoying a swift gallon of ale, appeared before a local magistrate for his over indulgences. His drunken frolic earned him a fine of 2/6d ($12^1/_2$p) which he recouped some weeks later when the same magistrate, obliged to use the ferry crossing, was taken only half way across the river, before the usual toll of 1d was dramatically raised (temporarily) to 2/6d! The magistrate felt that this was preferable to swimming the second half of the journey.

Trew's Weir

Beyond the attractive Port Royal Inn, which was once severely damaged by a freak tornado, the waters of the Exe gather ominous momentum. For those in peril on the water, danger signs warn of dire consequences ahead. If the Exe is in flood, the plunge over Trew's Weir can be quite spectacular but in time of drought persons with good balance can be seen traversing the weir without a problem. The weir was built in the early 1560s in order to create sufficient depth of water for the first Exeter Canal, engineered by John Trew.

The former Trew's Weir Paper Mill was an odd assortment of buildings, the oldest surviving one bearing the date 1780, although documented evidence first accounts for industry on this site in 1795. Robert Tipping built the cotton spinning mill initially and is believed to have employed some 300 men and women at one time. In 1812 this ceased as a cotton mill, only to re-open in 1834. As a child I fished there, keeping a watchful eye for the owner, then Mr Pitts, because fishing below the weir, in the mill tail, was private. I didn't want to upset him as I supplemented my pocket money by taking pramfuls of newspapers to the mill where, depending on the going rate, I received a reasonable return for my recycling efforts.

This mill and its immediate landscape have changed much in recent years. Today many of the mill buildings have been demolished for the building of the residential development of Trew's Mill Reach.

'The Match Factory' (Trew's Weir Court)

Any phillumenist embarking on an industrial archaeological safari to acquire new labels need not visit this spot as the name is believed to be a misnomer.

Although the oldest part of it dated back to 1774 its history is a bit of a puzzle. In the mid-nineteenth century it was named as Lower Mill on maps and flax was processed there. Tangible evidence of this were the troughs, which were utilised to remove the non-fibrous parts, once located near the Match Factory. After 1850 the building was temporarily used by the paper mill as a place for manufacturing paper bags and was also once used as stables. It also became a warehouse for Trew's Weir Paper Mill. Today, part of the 'Match Factory' building, shown here, has been demolished, and rebuilt as a housing development. The two blocks of garages look like miniature fire stations!

The Suspension Bridge

Crossing the Exe, always an obstacle, is possible for pedestrians at this point beside the Match Factory on a suspension bridge engineered in 1935.

The former Belle Isle sewage works, just south of this bridge, is now an attractive riverside park. The walk along the eastern side of the river will take you to Salmon Pool in about half a mile.

Salmon Pool

There is nothing pretentious about the name of Abbey Court, standing sentinel above St James' Weir. At this spot was the Priory of St James owned by Baldwin, Earl of Devon (and resident of Corfe Castle in Dorset) who established it in 1141 for a Prior and four monks. Although this has long gone, Priory High School still takes its name from it. Richard Duke, who resided at Mount Radford (a house demolished in 1902 which stood where Barnardo Road is now located), was responsible for pulling down the main buildings in 1760.

David Martin, an enthusiastic treasure hunter, has found many old coins on the opposite bank of the Exe. One possible reason for discovering such trove is the great number of people who used to cross the Exe at this point. It was common for people to bypass Exeter using Salmon Pool's ferry, which ran for hundreds of years. The main road from North Devon entered the Exeter area at Pennsylvania, followed the ridge of Polsloe Road to Livery Dole and headed for the Exe along the line of Barrack Road. Routes diverged beyond the ferry crossing point: one went south to link with the Port Way to the Teign; another climbed Haldon; whilst two other routes led towards Crediton and Moretonhampstead. Clapperbrook Lane, largely swallowed up by the Marsh Barton Trading Estate, was the link on the western side of the Exe. There was a refreshment hut on the west bank which closed in the early 1930s, having been gutted by fire, shortly after the ferry ceased.

Interestingly, since those old trade routes existed, proposed plans to bridge the Exe at Salmon Pool have been common. Thomas Sharp, in his plan *The Exeter Phoenix,* envisaged a route directly to Marsh Barton thus alleviating Exe Bridge. In more recent times another proposal was forcefully defeated by interested parties whose houses stood near the route of the proposed road. Salmon Pool is popular with local people as it is open space and a country park. Unofficial swimming takes place despite a low line of railings and a few prohibitory signs. When these lands were up for sale in July 1933 one of the selling points was that Salmon Pool would make an excellent venue for boating or even as a bathing pool. Also advocated for this proposed leisure centre were tennis courts and other facilities. At least today there is a 'kiddies' play park, playing fields, some maisonettes and the University of Plymouth's art faculty. In this vicinity, between Salmon Pool and Topsham Road, early Devon County Shows once took place. Residents of Salmon Pool Lane have found farmers' clay pipes in their gardens.

To the south much of the land belongs to Exeter University. These fields, which were once subject to frequent inundation, are known as Duck's Marsh playing fields. Technically this is an island as St James Leat is cut down its eastern margin. Lurking in its reedy waters are many large voracious pike, 'the freshwater shark', several being in excess of 20 pounds and capable of eating small dogs – so be careful if you go for a paddle!

The Exeter Canal

"Whenever you are passing, do drop in!" These were always the first words used by the host of the now defunct Double Locks Folk Club, beside Exeter Canal. The very thought of unintentionally entering the canal must send a shiver down the spine of any motorist contemplating a journey along the towpath. After one leaves the inn on a winter evening the stony silence of the deep waters is often made more sinister by the swirling mists. Even people who know the towpath are at risk – Mr Hutchings, a former lock-keeper at Double Locks, met an untimely watery death driving home one evening. An autopsy revealed no evidence of drinking on his part or on that of the two colleagues who drowned with him. He had made hundreds of journeys along the path and knew every twist and turn.

By contrast, on hot sunny Sundays the canal is anything but sinister, with people making it come alive. Families picnic along its banks, fathers and sons (and sometimes mothers and daughters) expectantly carry immense bags of fishing gear which would impress the most pugnacious pike, let alone the puniest perch. Joggers of all ages, sizes and shapes pant and pound along. Canoeists ply away laboriously whilst courting couples fall in ... that is, they fall in love with the beautiful views across Woodbury's Commons or to the tree-lined, magnificent scarp of the Haldon Hills. The canal is many things to many people. It has its moods and, like most old relics, has stories to tell, both past and present. Here are but a few facts and stories of what was Britain's first pound-lock canal.

A Brief Look at Exeter Canal's History

Before 1282 the River Exe was tidal as far as the cliffs in Bonhay Road and ships could dock at the natural shelf of the Quay. However, the Countess of Devon had other ideas and is alleged to have been responsible for a barrier placed across the river two miles below the City. Isabella de Fortibus truncated Exeter from the sea and usurped the trade, which was forced to pass through Topsham. She owned this port and enjoyed a greatly increased trade.

Countess Wear maintains its name derived from this action although the weir has long since gone. The City Fathers petitioned the King, who ordered a 30-foot gap in the weir, midstream, but soon after it appeared, Hugh de Courtenay, Earl of Devon, blocked it with stone and timber so effectively that it even caused flooding after heavy rain. Even though the City was given permission to remove it by Henry VIII, it was discovered that subsequent silting of the river had altered its profile to the extent that the river would never again be navigable up to the Quay.

And so it was in 1563 that John Trew, of Glamorgan, was engaged to engineer a route towards it. The initial idea was to cut along the eastern side of the Exe but preliminary investigations revealed that the nature of the rocks would have provided tough excavating. The west side was selected, its alluvial soils much more amenable, and by 1566 the first pound-lock canal in Britain had been built. It was 3,120 yards long, 3 feet deep and 16 feet wide. To raise the £5,000 necessary, churches in Exeter contributed part of their gold and silver plate to subsidise the council funds. The canal was not the success that the Corporation had hoped that it would be. They had shrewdly inserted a clause in John Trew's contract, that at all times ten-ton vessels should be able to use the canal, a situation which was rarely possible. Trew made little profit from his canal but his name has been immortalised in Trew's Weir where his canal began.

The Canal continued to exasperate its users, with trade declining as a result of tediously long journeys to reach Exeter. The authorities employed William Bayley to widen, deepen and lengthen the canal in 1698. This was to facilitate an easier shipment of Exeter's many manufactures. After a year of work on this project Bayley fled, having embezzled the funds. It was another 26 years before the work was done, the canal now 4 miles long, 60 feet wide and 10 feet deep – good value for the £20,000 that it cost. Unfortunately Exeter's prime importance as a centre of the wool trade declined, with the canal attracting fewer 150-ton vessels each year.

The growth in the use of coal for industrial purposes from 1791 meant the canal enjoyed a rebirth. The famous engineer James Green advised the Corporation to extend the canal, in 1827, to its present length of just over 5 miles. Its new outlet into the Exe Estuary was now at Turf. Larger vessels were accommodated as the 90 feet wide, 14 feet deep canal had plenty of traffic along it until the middle of the nineteenth century. The Canal Basin was added in 1830 and was known as the New Cut for many years. After that time trade again dwindled and large debts were amassed as the upkeep of costs exceeded the revenue.

Canal Trade

Although it is now purely academic, it is interesting to observe that English vessels using the canal did not require a pilot whereas foreign vessels had to have one. The cargoes they brought included petrol, timber, coal, cement, oil, grain, onions, apples, oats, potatoes, fertiliser and a lot of slag. The range of ports which traded with Exeter until recent years was impressive: Walkdon, Norssundet, St Malo, Åbo, Dieppe, Le Guildo, Appingedam, Rotterdam, Le Tréport, St Vaast la Houge being just some of them. However, most of the trade was inter-coastal.

These vessels brought in not only their cargoes but also some really unusual characters. French vessels carrying onions unloaded at the Basin. The cargo was complete with onion sellers and their bicycles all stored in a warehouse where 'Onion

Johnnies' slept outstretched upon their wares – enough to bring tears to your eyes! These enterprising men strung their onions and took them around Exeter's streets until they were all sold. Needless to say on windy days one knew they were coming long before their familiar cries could be heard.

Years ago the bridge-keeper at the Countess Wear Swing Bridge was officially Mr Shorland of Exminster. However, it was his sister, Hannah, who was most often seen in attendance at openings of the bridge. She was a woman who did not need equality of opportunity in order to assert herself. Her forthright and direct approach was not always appreciated by passing sailors or by queues of motorists inconvenienced by the bridge opening. Queues of impatient motorists also incurred the wrath of this lady if they dared to hoot their displeasure. She lived with her cat in a tied cottage beside the Swing Bridge. When the bridge was to be opened she would bring traffic to a standstill with red flags. These were left either side of the bridge in a small umbrella-type stand. At regular intervals she came up and swept the main road, one of the busiest in England, removing dust and litter so that the white lines in the middle of the road were the best kept in the land. Despite her natural eccentricity and tendency towards an aggressive approach she was highly thought of by those who knew her well. There are now two bridges – one a lifting span – and when they are to be opened the news is spread on the local radio station by the police.

Other buildings which have disappeared from this area are the limekilns by the canal and an adjacent row of cottages where the workers lived.

Beside the canal are the flat lands known as Exminster Marsh, the only extensive level area in Devon. During the war it was selected for training parachutists for landings in Northern France and Belgium – a similar landscape. Unfortunately for them, many parachutists landed feet first in tanks – at the sewage works!

A rather bizarre discovery was made by a former lock-keeper of the Double Locks, whose patch extended to the limekilns, in the 1930s. Whilst patrolling he noticed a brown parcel near to the water's edge. When unravelled a human leg was found inside. Further searching revealed another packaged leg. Despite dredging and a thorough search by divers, no other parts of the body could be found. The police theory was that a medical student must have been disposing of his research material.

The Towpath

In the past there were three stables along the canal: at the Canal Yard near the City Basin, at Double Locks and at Turf. The last horse used was 'Captain', stabled at Double Locks and led by its owner George Bye.

At Double Locks, where the heavy lock gates have to be opened by heaving balance beams, there used to be this interesting war relic. When the gate beams became faulty they were replaced by sections of the mainmast of HMS *Exeter*, later sunk in the Battle of the Java Sea. The mast had been presented to the City on its last refit and a bronze plaque gave the details of the presentation.

The Former Maritime Museum

The International Sailing Craft Association, or more aptly 'ISCA' (Exeter's Roman name was *Isca Dumnoniorum*), were once responsible for the vast collection of craft from all corners of the world. The Maritime Museum established itself as a leading national and international tourist attraction. Larger craft, including tugs like the *St Canute* (*St Knud* when she worked out of the port of Odense from 1931) and the pearling dhow given by the Ruler of Bahrain, were moored in the Basin whilst

smaller craft were housed in warehouses. The semi-derelict Canal Basin, where it was formerly located, was brought back to life by this museum. In its life of about three decades it enjoyed many highs and lows. Some will remember Sir Alec Rose who was rowed up the canal by the Exeter Sea Cadets as part of an Open Day on 27 June 1969. The boat on which he was carried had been built for the film *A Man for All Seasons* (1966), which had been written by Sir Robert Bolt, once a schoolmaster at Bishopsteignton. Others will remember certain vessels like the *Bedford* lifeboat, 'moored' under the old fish market on the Quay and part of the scenery for many years.

Many people were dumbfounded, even distraught, in 1997 to see the collection of boats sold and disbanded. There are those who are still angry and puzzled as to why more wasn't done to keep it in Exeter, particularly as it was in a part of the city where tourism was being actively encouraged and developed. Part of this lovingly assembled collection was shipped to Bristol whilst the rest was carried to the east coast port of Lowestoft.

Exeter has lost a valuable educational resource and a unique tourist attraction. Generations of schoolchildren learnt much about the sea, trade and other countries from the Maritime Museum. Sadly, it ran into financial problems which resulted in its ultimate closure. Hopefully in years to come, there may be something new and wonderful here and not just more offices, flats or houses!

The Lost Streams of Exeter

In Devon almost every dip, combe, depression or valley bears a stream but in Exeter similar hollows appear to be dry. Within Exeter's confines are many brooks and streams which still flow, but now are many feet beneath the surface. Undoubtedly they are all streams which, before the development of Exeter as a Roman town, contained a healthy fish population. It is safe to assume that many were the spawning grounds for game fish like trout and salmon. Some of these streams have been radically altered within living memory and places where I caught trout as a boy are now underground storm sewers. It is a constructive suggestion for architects and planners, when they design their new housing sites or industrial estates, that if their territory is blessed by a stream, however insignificant, they should adapt it into their landscaping programme. Streams, if ponded or landscaped, can be integrated into the environment successfully. The Taddiforde Brook at the University of Exeter is a good example of a stream which has been landscaped to enhance the surroundings.

Sadly, Exeter has not always been as 'ever faithful' to its streams as it has been to Royalty. This section of the book examines, only briefly, the situation of its waterways, some sentenced to remain in cavern-like storm sewers beneath a concrete and tarmac jungle.

The Coombe Brook

This stream was only about 500 yards long yet, within this extremely short distance, managed to drop over 40 feet in height from its springs, now the site of Exeter Cathedral, into the area of the Quay. Coombe Street ('combe' is a Celtic word meaning 'valley') takes its name from this stream. Its dip can be seen as a marked change of slope at the bottom of South Street. After heavy rain the stream flowing down from the site of Palace Gate must have been an impressive spectacle but was also something of a nuisance. Therefore it was covered over, probably early in the thirteenth century.

The Shit Brook, or the Barnfield Brook

This stream, about a mile in length, started in the present day Newtown area at Chute Street, which is a polite derivation of the name. The stream was fast flowing and on the seaward side of the City. This meant that it was well suited for the removal of human waste, which it did from Saxon times onwards, hence its name. In hot weather the stream stenched as the flow was stifled. Periodic downpours were regarded as a blessing as nature flushed this foul watercourse.

To envisage its route has now been made difficult by developers who, at different times, have shifted enormous amounts of earth and rock, resulting in the present-day topography. Heavitree Road, near the Paris Street roundabout, has been built up by several feet. Paris Street (formerly called Shitbrook Street) ran down to it. Following the cholera epidemic of 1832, which claimed hundreds of lives in Exeter, the brook was culverted.

In 1977 the late David Rees, a former lecturer at St Luke's College, published *The Ferryman,* an excellent novel based on this epidemic. He used, as source material, the writings of one of the city's doctors who treated the sick and dying at that terrible time.

More earth-shifting in Barnfield Road prevents the valley of this stream being recognised near 'Althelstan's Dyke'. The stream flowed through Bull Meadow, crossed beneath Holloway Street into the area long known as Larkbeare, and issued into the river at the bottom of Colleton Hill.

Crolditch

Although not strictly a stream, 'Crolditch' was a double ditch used first by the Romans for much the same purpose as the Barnfield Brook. It stretched from Southernhay to the Water Gate and, when used, bore the waters of a spring which was probably culverted.

Close to those beautifully laid out lawns and flower beds, which act as an island between Southernhay East and West, were two pools known as Southernhay Pools. In 1659 their popularity reached an all-time low with plenty of public dissent as these pools were: "complayned to bee very dangerous to people passing by and noysome by reason of dead horses and other filth cast into the same."

Noysome meant 'smelling'. These were duly filled in so that today when folk sunbathe in their lunch breaks on these lawns they would never suspect what a gruesome mixture lies beneath them.

The Long Brook

The Long Brook shares several similarities with the Barnfield Brook. It flowed parallel with it, was about the same length, is now underground (completely since 1843), and likewise is difficult to envisage owing to developers shaping the relief to suit their own needs. The Long Brook had two main sources; one began near St Sidwell's School whilst another issued from beneath the site of the large Debenhams store. The first of these springs is visibly reinforced in the name of Well Street. Where Central Station now stands the stream was sufficiently wide and deep to enable young lads to bathe. It continued beneath the site of the Iron Bridge and joined the river in Bonhay Road. It still flows many feet below the ground but can be seen at the bottom of Exe Street beneath the road.

The Alphin Brook

The largest of the streams entering the Exe at Exeter is the Alphin Brook which rises about 5 miles to the west near Pathfinder Village. It has two main tributaries – the Nadder Brook, which rises in the hills near Whitestone, and the Fordland Brook which flows through Ide. These streams have quite sharp profiles in their upper courses. After prolonged heavy rain their combined swollen flows descend upon the low-lying areas of Alphington and have caused much watery grief in the past. In the early 1960s the Alphin Brook caused so many problems in the Marsh Barton area that on several occasions the workforce on the industrial estate were forced to evacuate their buildings. At a Cadbury and Fry depot workers were rescued from the roofs of the single-storey building by amphibious army vehicles based at Wyvern Barracks. As a result of these floods, and the planned growth of building at Alphington, it was deemed necessary to canalise the lower Alphin Brook within concrete banks to avoid any further problems. These banks have eventually 'greened-up' to blend in better with the landscape.

The lower valley of this stream system has witnessed many changes. Quiet spots like Clark's Road, where for decades little boys caught minnows, stone loach or bullheads, have lost their country brook atmosphere when the Pocombe Bridge link was built through the valley. Villagers at Ide were so incensed at this intrusion that they erected a gravestone commemorating the death of the valley. As a child I spent many hours fishing with a net at a point on the Alphin Brook at Rolls Bridge Farm. The fields beside the stream where my friends and I improvised games of football using jerseys as goalposts, are now part of the hard shoulder of the A30. However, such fond memories need to be weighed up against the situation where the volume of traffic destined to pass through Alphington would have continued to make life a nightmare for locals and travellers alike. Everything has a price!

The Wonford Brook

Another brook which starts in the hills to the north of Exeter, which has seen even greater change, is the Wonford Brook.

This is a veritable Amazon of a stream compared to some of the others in this chapter. It is all of 4 miles long, starts in mountainous hills about 400 feet above sea level, and has numerous tributaries. Because of these connecting rivulets there arises a problem of identity, as so many names appear to have been bestowed upon it. In its upper reaches one of the two main feeders bears the name Mincinglake. This is an old name, derived from ecclesiastical ties with a priory which existed close to Beacon Lane, meaning literally 'nun's stream'. The other main feeder rises above Beacon Heath and drops down through Whipton Village. As the streams descend from these hills in a trickle-like fashion they gather momentum as other flows are added. A spring which rises in Exeter Cemetery flows to join the main course near Heavitree Bridge. Another tributary has its own ' birthplace' near the former maternity home of Mowbray in Butts Road. It flows through the old village of Wonford to link with the main stream at Wonford Playing Fields. Here the stream is called the Wonford Brook but in a few yards changes name again to assume the title of North Brook, where it passes through the approach golf course of the same name, and the grounds of Exeter Crematorium. To say that the stream itself has died is an understatement. It was not many years ago when this stream flowed through green meadows and orchards. Families made outings into the countryside, just outside Exeter, to hold picnics beside its clear waters. The stream was abundant in small fishes – brook trout were a common sight and even salmon were seen at times.

Today the growth of suburban Exeter has totally changed the stream. Where orchards once scented the air, houses impose on the privacy of the brook. No thought was given to the use of the stream as a potentially attractive feature to set off the dwellings in roads like Brookway and Leypark Road. Indeed houses were built facing away from it and the stream took on an unattractive, abandoned appearance.

When the dustbin men went on strike in the 1970s, life began to be difficult for Whiptonians and the stream became the dumping place for all manner of unwanted rubbish – and this has continued to be the case ever since.

However, it would be wrong to portray the stream as an innocent victim as in times of storm the stream flooded areas of Whipton to a depth of several feet, causing much damage. Two reasons account for this: the stream flows though New Red Sandstone rocks which are easily eroded when the river is in spate, and the Whipton Brook was constantly in spate because all the rain waters falling in the catchment area were channelled quickly into it by a network of drains using the stream as a storm sewer!

To remedy this, some sections of the stream were canalised, straightened to flow submissively through concrete corridors, whilst in other places the stream was put underground. In other problem places loose banks have been either reinforced or shored up by carefully placed gabions.

The quasi-end product is a lamentable flow of water, devoid of any significant fish population, slowly becoming another 'lost' stream. How long will people remember to ask for 'Heavitree Bridge' when taking a bus ride to this part of the City, and how many people will tell their children the reason for this place-name?

The Pin Brook

It begins in Fairy Dell and then the romance ends! This stream gives its name to Pinhoe, which it shyly passes on its way to its confluence with the River Clyst. It bubbles and gurgles manfully enough down to Heath Barton at the foot of Cheynegate Lane, but then is dwarfed by mountains of bricks – 'The Westbrick Range'. It creeps beneath Pinhoe Road and skirts what is now a field but may not be for long. The massive Monkerton estate borders its banks as it leaves the present edge of urban Exeter to sluggishly meander its way to the Clyst.

The Taddiforde Brook

This stream flows though what most local people term the Hoopern Valley. As the University of Exeter is adjacent to the stream the advantages of landscaping and adaptation are visible. The upper parts of the brook are ponded and have been stocked with fish and many species of duck. On any fine Sunday afternoon, even in midwinter, you will find people strolling around enjoying the semi-rural surroundings. Out of all the streams in Exeter this is the only one that has retained some element of respect – obviously the result of a good University education!

Exeter Floods

Most of the streams and rivers around Exeter have been liable to flood in the past. The Wonford Brook did great damage at Whipton, Wonford and Heavitree Bridge in 1972. The Alphin, or Ide, Brook's wanderings have been revealed elsewhere in

this book. The River Clyst (meaning 'clear stream') floods its flat meadows near Sowton and Clyst St Mary almost every year. However, it is the River Exe which has created the most human misery by inundating the nether area of Exeter, particularly St Thomas and Exwick, on many occasions in the past.

The first fluvial indiscretions sufficient in strength to remove substantial buildings occurred in 1403 when the Church of St Thomas the Martyr was washed away. Hours later a much earler 'edition' Exe Bridge was also washed away in the same flood. Traditionally St Thomas has been a 'wet' area. Most of the neat rows of Victorian houses are built on reclaimed swamp land, which may account for many showing signs of subsidence as the old extensions drift away from the main parts of the dwellings. The photographs depict floods at Cowick Street (1960) and at nearby Okehampton Place (1954). The car shown did not leak even though the flood waters nearly submerged it!

The 1960 floods were the worst to occur in living memory. A boy, bored by his enforced stay at home, caught a trout by angling from his upstairs window in Clinton Street.

A short distance away at the Royal Oak in Okehampton Street, a full barrel of beer was washed down the Exe. It disappeared on 27 October 1960 and was picked up by HMS *Highburton* on 8 December, seven miles east of Portland. It was duly returned and the brewery showed their appreciation by entertaining the crew. The beer barrel now resides in the public bar serving as a seat. A brass plate commemorates its unusual story.

Two people trapped by the fast-rising flood waters sought refuge in Emmanuel Church. The safest place was the pulpit, where a wait of a few hours was ended by a rowing-boat floating up the aisle to make the rescue.

The toll on families living in the low-lying parts of Exwick, St Thomas and Exe Island (shown here) was devastating. Possessions and property damage amounted to

a colossal sum. The torrent through some streets was so powerful that it turned motor cars over and washed them away. The only blessing was that no loss of human life could be directly attributed to the floods. Today the chance of such events repeating themselves has been greatly reduced by a number of flood prevention schemes.

Valley Parks

A more enlightened approach has been shown in three of the small valleys around Exeter. Duryard (Pennsylvania) and Ludwell valleys have been preserved from house-building along with the upper Mincinglake Valley – and have been converted into valley parks for recreation purposes. These schemes are only part of a strategy for improving recreational facilities in this leisure and pleasure city – perhaps all is not yet lost.

Villages Within Exeter

Logic seems to suggest that if a town has many natural locational advantages, it will grow and, as we have already seen, the earliest settlement developed close to the lowest fording point on the Exe. Exeter is also in the centre of an agricultural region. Its markets thrive on the business of dairy farmers from the Culm Measures country to the north and west of the City, from the hill farms of Dartmoor and Exmoor, from the arable areas of the New Red Sandstone soils to the south-east of Exeter, and from the many market gardens around the City.

Routes converge on Exeter as the shape of the land in Devon necessitates that both road and rail routes funnel towards the City. The M5 closely follows the Culm Valley for many miles, and ends on the City's outskirts to become a very fast 'cartrack' known as the 'Devon Expressway' (A38). The other major route is the ever-busy A30, which once passed through the centre of Exeter but now skirts the city. Many other A-class roads converge on Exeter to ensure that it's rarely short of the 'delights' of traffic congestion.

If you add in the other 'functions' of Exeter it is clear that here is a city which has obviously grown considerably. For Exeter is the cultural, educational, business, commercial, shopping, religious, sporting and tourist centre of the region. Thus from its humble beginnings, around a perilous crossing place on the Exe, it has extended outwards to absorb districts and villages which were once individual settlements but have now almost lost their own identity. This has inevitably changed the scenery. This view of Rosebarn Lane is a fine example, just one lane of many in Exeter to succumb to the urban onslaught. Every village, town and city has its Rosebarn Lanes!

The relentless and constant growth of building in Exeter meant that the villages of Whipton, Heavitree, Countess Wear, St Thomas and Exwick have been swallowed up. The rural atmosphere of these settlements has disappeared as the building invasion has surrounded them. It can be fun to imagine what these places looked like at different times in the past. Each district has managed to retain some individuality owing to their own shopping areas which, along with their churches, have engendered a sense of pride and belonging. Even postal codes have not managed to sway folk away from including their former village names when stating addresses. As each of these settlements is different, here is but a glimpse of them in former days.

WHIPTON

Whipton derives from 'Wippa's farm', a Saxon who owned the land some 1,200 years ago. There are few signs of farms today as Exeter has encompassed this village within its City boundaries. The nucleus of the original village was clustered around the crossroads of Whipton Village Road and Summer Lane. The harmless-looking

stream, now penned by concrete banks, was, as we have already seen, a constant threat in winter-time causing frequent flooding.

Maps reveal clearly how Whipton has been absorbed as a suburb of Exeter but it has a past of its own. The Tithe Map of 1844 shows the agricultural nature of this small settlement of less than 100 folk. Exeter's largest council house estate of Whipton Barton stands on former pasture land on the heights of Thornpark Rise. The lower, more fertile slopes were blessed with sweet smelling blossoms and apple trees, and the stream was well stocked with Devon minnows and trout. With Exeter penned back by the Exeter-to-Exmouth branch railway line, Exonians would visit Whipton and its immediate countryside, largely owned by Lord Poltimore, for their perambulations.

Whipton Halt

Whiptonians had their own railway station at the turn of the century. This was sited at Whipton Bridge in Summer Lane, adjacent to the field where the Devon County Show used to take place before moving out to Westpoint at Clyst St Mary. Whipton Halt provided a useful means for people to get to 'nearby' Exeter. Eventually buses replaced steam travel, although in 1953 there was talk of opening a station at a point where the Exeter by-pass crosses the Exmouth Branch line. Presumably, had it been opened, it would have been called Hill Barton Halt.

Murder Most Foul

The principal building of Whipton was generally regarded as Whipton Barton House, part of a large farm. In 1953 an *Express and Echo* report stated:

"Whipton Barton House, its garden and other parts of the house are being preserved ... [it] is one of the features remaining to remind us of the old atmosphere, it will indeed be a sort of oasis." Alas, an historic drought has seen this particular oasis, on the south side of the Vaughan Road and Pinhoe Road junction, disappear. This picture shows its demolition.

In the past it had many owners including one unfortunate who was murdered. In 1611 those lands belonged to the Petre family. One January afternoon Will Petre rode with Edward and John Drew, of Killerton, into Exeter. They visited many inns including the Dolphin Inn and the Bear Inn, near South Street. Sir Edward Seymour, of Berry Pomeroy House, borrowed some gold from them to play cards. At a time believed to be between 7 and 8 p.m. the trio of friends left to return home. Their route took them through the East Gate along St Sidwells. Beyond this point the facts are open to speculation but poor Will Petre was murdered by a single blow to the head. His body was found near St Anne's Chapel in what is today known as Blackboy Road.

The witness who claimed that Edward Drew had said, "He rideth fast, but I will give him a nick before he gets home," must have thought he was condemning the man to the hangman's noose. Fortunately for Edward his father was an important lawyer, which probably accounts for his cheating the gallows. Some reports say that Edward was smuggled out of the country whilst others say he retired to Broadclyst where he spent the rest of his life.

Whipton Names

Until 1946 the Barton (meaning 'corn farm') was owned by Farmer Alford. The Council purchased the land to build a large estate. The former fields of Leypark, Headland, Endfield and Thornpark gave their names to roads which are built upon them today. Farmer Alford is represented by Alford Close.

Fire!

The event which almost destroyed the heart of Whipton in June 1895 was a great fire. It was so fierce that it burned houses on both sides of the main road. Traffic trying to reach Exeter market had to be diverted. The holocaust completely gutted five houses (most of which were insured in the Commercial Union) and did great damage.

The fire was spotted by a farmer en route to market at 6.50 a.m. By 7.10 a.m. the Exeter brigade, with its four-horse-power carriage, had arrived. Their efforts to stop the conflagration were hindered by the lack of water as Whipton in 1895 was not yet on the mains supply. However, behind All Saints Church were two ponds which provided an improvised supply. The Half Moon Hotel was threatened a few times but thanks to a man named Crews, who stationed himself on the roof with bucketfuls of water, the inn survived. The Half Moon was formerly an important eighteenth and nineteenth-century coaching house on the Exeter–Bristol run. Until 1891 it traded under the name of the Star Inn.

Other brigades came to give assistance, including those of Heavitree and St Thomas. Ten prized pigeons were rescued, although one was so badly damaged it had to have its neck wrung.

HEAVITREE

In Georgian and Victorian times Heavitree established itself as an upper class residential village, away from Exeter socially as well as locationally. As recently as 1831 well-to-do ladies were conveyed in sedan chairs to parties. The outbreak of cholera the following year was particularly devastating as Heavitree lay on a direct route as the epidemic spread.

As both Exeter and Heavitree grew in the nineteenth century it became inevitable that the large village of Heavitree would become a part of Exeter and in 1911 there were moves afoot to absorb Heavitree. The residential folk of Heavitree attempted to resist this as it was in their own interest to avoid paying increased rates demands. However, this was all to no avail as Mr Kendall King, Mayor of Exeter in 1913, became the first Mayor of Greater Exeter with the addition of Heavitree Ward. Beatrix F. Cresswell later added these philosophical thoughts on the matter: "It is not absorbed into Exeter, it is only added as a brighter jewel to Exeter's crown!"

Heavitree Executions

Criminals who journeyed to Heavitree many generations ago would, no doubt, have preferred not to for it was on the edge of this large parish that they involuntarily departed this mortal coil. The first place of execution until 1531 was at Livery Dole, close to the meeting place of Polsloe Road and Heavitree Road, a hilltop site. The last execution there was that of Thomas Benet who was burnt at the stake for his religious beliefs. Accounts of his execution suggest that it was a particularly brutal affair.

Thomas Benet had allowed one of his sons to attach a message to the West Door of Exeter Cathedral which proclaimed that, "The Pope is Anti-Christ and we ought to worship God only, and no saints!" For this act of heresy Thomas was chained to the stake. Several people encouraged him to deny such statements but this he stubbornly refused to do. John Burnthouse was so greatly angered that he thrust a burning furze-bush into Benet's mouth saying "Pray to our Lady or by God I will make thee do it!" This torturous act only managed to succeed in producing this response, "Alas Sir, trouble me not." Whereupon as the pyre was lit he quietly prayed until his life ebbed away. Two monuments have been erected to his memory, the Almshouses at Livery Dole and a 20-foot-high pillar of Dartmoor granite at Martyrs Memorial Corner in Denmark Road, Exeter, which was paid for in 1909 by public subscription.

In 1851, when the site for the present Almshouses at Livery Dole was being excavated, the iron ring which encircled the victims' bodies and the chain which tied them to the stake were unearthed.

It is probable that the Lords of Heavitree and Wonford had the right to have the gallows upon their manors. The new site for executions was two miles from Exeter at 'Ringwell', at the other end of the parish. The name exists today in Ringswell Avenue, which was extremely close to the gallows sited on a point where the Sidmouth Road rises from Honiton Road. In 1926 a gruesome collection of skeletons was unearthed at this point. Further finds at 125 Honiton Road were made in 1973. It was an accepted practice to bury the dead in the environs of the scaffold.

The condemned prisoners were brought from Exeter on a huge horse-drawn cart. They sat on their coffins whilst making this journey from the County Gaol. At Heavitree Bridge a small spring which issued from the side of the hill (Quarry Lane) was where the condemned people took their last drink. Although the last executions took place at this spot in 1802, people on buses still ask for 'The Gallows', it being a name in common usage even today. The nearby bridge carrying the Exeter By pass over Honiton Road is called Gallows Bridge.

Heavitree Brewery

In a sense 'Heavitree Brewery' is one with no beer. They stopped brewing their own ales in 1970 to receive in their stead draught supplies from Whitbread. Thirty people were made redundant as Exeter's last working brewery ceased brewing. It had large premises in Church Street but moved out. The old brewery buildings were bulldozed and the company moved out to Trood House on the outskirts of Exeter, near Matford. The firm still manages many pubs in the area. More about them can be discovered in *Heavitree of Yesteryear*, a book of past pictures from in and around the parish.

Heavitree Races

These meetings took place in late Victorian times and were a traditional event held in September. In 1880 thousands of race-goers made their way to the 'Point-to-Point' course which was about $1^1/_2$ miles long. It covered much of the land where St Luke's High School (which opened in 1953 as 'Vincent Thompson') is now located. The course also included much of the Hill Barton area, a part of the city where there is much new housing spreading beyond the route of the By pass (opened in 1936). The boundary of the 'race-course' was the railway branch line to Exmouth. An 'ordinary' is a meal following a race event and this was always celebrated in one of the many Heavitree pubs.

COUNTESS WEAR

The spelling of 'Wear' has caused much debate down the years because this 'village' takes its name from the water barrier built across the Exe and there is only one way to spell 'weir'. The original village is beside the Exe and the spread of this suburb remains on the north-east side of the Exe for practical reasons. The marshes and flat flood plain beyond the river look ominously upstream because they can see the southward encroachment of the apparently ever-growing Marsh Barton estate.

Traffic

Residential and industrial growth and the vastly increased incidence of car ownership has ensured that Countess Wear gets far more than its fair share of traffic. There was a dip in traffic flow after the opening of the M5 but this was only a lull and the situation gets ever worse. Topsham Road becomes a continuous snake of traffic into Exeter early each morning, and a veritable anaconda on its ebb each evening. On wet summer days the flood of traffic is swollen by the mass of holidaymakers, pouring into Exeter, 'making the most' of Britain's inclement climate.

The Exeter By pass, built and opened in 1936 as something of a 'freeway', became nationally notorious for its nose-to-tail queues. On peak summer Saturdays it was customary to see tail-backs stretching its entire length. Journeys from Taunton to Torquay frequently took seven hours, and caused a lot of bad language. You can imagine the reaction when the Canal Swing Bridge was opened to allow ships to pass through at such times! Chris Barrie, alias 'Gordon Brittas' or 'Rimmer', included rare footage of the Exeter By pass as it was the 1950s in a BBC video called *Motoring Wheel Nuts*, and featured Mr Shorland, albeit momentarily, at the Swing Bridge. It also showed newspaper vendors walking along the endless queue of traffic selling their wares.

Key:

A *Countess Wear village*	***D*** *Crematorium*
B *Countess Wear Bridge*	***E*** *Countess Wear Mill*
C *Glasshouse Cut*	***F*** *Topsham Road*

Robert Davy – A Countess Wear Shipbuilder

Robert Davy was a shipbuilder at Countess Wear and achieved great fame for his exploits. His years spanned an important time in England's maritime history – he was born in 1762 and died in 1862 and although it appears, at first glance, that he made it to the great age of 100, it's sad to relate that he fell short of becoming a centenarian by just under two months.

James Davy, his father, bought Wear Barton, on the south side of Glasshouse Lane, and initially pursued agricultural activities but soon diversified, adding a quay and limekilns at Countess Wear village, and promptly went to live there. His livelihood was boosted by his coal business based on coastal trade from the north-east.

Robert took over in 1790. He utilised a small man-made channel, known then as 'Glasshouse Cut', either side of Countess Wear Bridge, for his boat building exploits. Amazingly vessels of over 600 tons were launched there, albeit in a strange fashion. The shallow Exe was not suited to conventional launchings even at the highest of Spring tides so a system evolved.where ships were raised on floating casks, chained to kegs, and pulled into deeper waters. The largest ship ever built in the Exe Estuary is thought to be the *Caroline* which came from the yard of Mr Davy in this fashion.

In 1802 Robert Davy, after a disagreement, moved a short distance up river to continue his work. The frustration of difficult launchings then led him to invest in a yard at the northern end of Topsham. In the wars with France he earned a reputation for meeting orders on time. This meant bonus payments and further orders, which lined his pockets and made him a wealthy man.

Robert's strength was his ability to adapt to new spheres of influence. He traded in the selling of bar iron and manufactured chain cables and anchors. Like his father, he was a coal merchant, limeburner and farmer. Although dogged by poor sight, which bordered on total blindness for long periods, Robert kept active. He involved himself in improving aspects of the local environment that he felt were wrong and to keep fit he walked 10 to 20 miles each day escorted by a boy. This he did for many years until his legs became weak. Refusing to lie down and die, he purchased a carriage in 1840, and with his one good eye saw to it that the local poor and infirm were given help and financial assistance. This is poignantly illustrated by his removal of the workhouse at Topsham. He invested the poor with sufficient funds not to require such basic institutional benevolence. This great local man finally succumbed and is buried at Clyst St Mary. Further details, for those with a thirst for historic liquor, can be gleaned from Topsham Museum where a biography, written by his youngest son, Francis, can be seen.

The Glasshouse

The history of glass making in Britain is not altogether clear, one might even say frosted. 'Ravenscroft' established the first glasshouse in the Savoy, London, in 1673. Within 25 years no less than 80 sprang up around the country, one of them being at Countess Wear in Devon, the same one giving its name to Glasshouse Lane. Its tower stood at the western end of the lane but was damaged in a storm when lightning struck it, probably about 1777.

An ingenious method was used to topple it. A short distance above the ground some timbers were wedged beneath this construction. These were set ablaze so that when they burnt through the tower came tumbling down. The garden wall today contains many of the bricks from it. Their distinct colour is attributed to the foreign clays which were used when firing them. Like many buildings and walls in the Countess Wear and Topsham area they were built from materials imported only as ballast in ships trading out of the Exe.

The death knell for many glasshouses was the prohibition of using wood for firing the furnace. This particular Glasshouse possibly used 'coal' or 'culm' mined from Duryard Wood (now the University campus), which had been made available by the City of Exeter in 1698.

The Mill in Mill Lane

Another interesting building at Countess Wear is the old mill which gives its name to Mill Lane. This edifice is surrounded by vegetation, giving it a sinister appearance. Pupils from a nearby school are warned that it is haunted, which helps to prevent them from exploring it whilst on their cross-country runs. Its history has caused some debate. Some believe that from 1658 it operated as a grist mill, whilst others suggest that its original function was as a woollen and cloth mill. In 1704 it switched to paper making, and was one of many found on or near the Exe. It specialised in quality paper made from rags. In 1816 this large mill was destroyed by fire but like the Phoenix rose from the ashes and prospered again. At its peak, about 1840, some 200 or so workers were employed. The influence of the Industrial Revolution reached this part of the country and the mill changed with the times, converting to steam power. However, the consumption of large amounts of coal eventually contributed to the mill's closure in 1885. In 1886 it was acquired by the local authority as a site for producing electricity, even though it was never developed for such a purpose. However, if you want to see it in all its glory, all you have to do is visit the excellent, but seasonal, Topsham Museum where there is a scale model of it. It was presented to the museum by a Countess Wear resident and is believed to have been the work of an apprentice employed at the mill in about 1860.

Crematorium and Golf Course(s)

Near the Mill are the grounds of the Crematorium, sadly the last rendezvous for many. The gardens, which are beautiful, provide a fitting place for final farewells.

Nearby a scene of stark contrast is evident as would-be golfers tackle the Approach Golf Course at Northbrook with varying degrees of success. In the drought years of the 1970s the second half of the course was rendered unplayable as the ground was so hard that it was impossible to hold the ball on any of the hillside greens – even the slightest touch produced a long walk, downhill. On the plus side, anyone who always managed to land in the North Brook whilst negotiating holes one and six had the advantage of an almost dried-up stream, making the inevitable and regular retrieval of balls an easier task.

Within the district of Countess Wear is a much more dignified golf course, a proper one, where golfers possess far different handicaps than those at Northbrook. The course was opened after a group of influential businessmen got together to buy Wear House from the Bradshaw family. They found that they were ineligible to join the existing nine-hole course, established in 1895, on the highest hills of Pennsylvania. They therefore decided to create their own and employed the famous golf course architect, James Braid, to design and build one on much more level and less wind-blown or rain-lashed lowlands. The course, now the Exeter Golf & Country Club, has established itself as a fine venue for this Royal and Ancient game. The only hiccough in its history was the use of the course as a war time airfield. Reports after the war suggested that it was unlikely golf would ever be played there again, so extensive was the damage caused at that time. Seven of the pre-Second World War holes were lost to the US Navy and a depot was later developed there by the Admiralty, who remained there until the 1990s. The Club acquired other adjacent land and James Braid's course was adapted, but even he would be amazed to see the range and extent of facilities now available to members.

Those first golf links at Pennsylvania, beside the Roman Signal Station, hosted other festivities which included Bonfire Night firework displays accompanied by local brass bands. It is probable the music was played breathlessly as the climb to this early venue was both long and steep.

EXWICK

'The dairy farm by the Exe' is the translation of Exwick, as a place-name. Today there is little rural flavour about the settlement as its 'village' has been invaded by a massive modern housing development. The pastures of Exwick must have exhausted those who tended them. The hillsides are almost cliff-like, whilst the land beside the Exe was too flat, poorly drained and frequently inundated. Those who lived there were aware of these shortcomings and sited their cottages on the valley side.

Two other old hamlets, which were also in the parish of St Thomas, were Foghay, a half mile to the north and Foxhays, a quarter of a mile to the south. Foghay has disappeared in the mists of time but Foxhayes has grown.

From the old photograph above Kinnerton Way, it is fun to speculate where the team of horses would be in the present day, a sort of 'spot the hoof' competition.

It is not surprising, with so much water flowing past Exwick, that it should once have had so many water-driven mills. For several centuries it was the provider of flour for Exeter's millers. Exwick Flour Mill was rebuilt in 1886 to use newly invented machinery but closed in 1958 to become a store. When the first edition of this book was published 'Mother's Pride' occupied large premises near St David's Station's level crossing but now houses occupy the site. As a pupil, in the early 1960s, at the former Episcopal SM School, in Mount Dinham, we were obliged to traipse down to a very different-looking Exwick Playing Fields for our games lessons. The route took us between a 'leat' and the back of this factory and one can never forget that smell. The leat or canal, which I fished at that time, went in the construction of the flood alleviation scheme. It was originally proposed to extend the Exeter Canal to Crediton and then on into West Devon. The valley of the Yeo or Creedy (meaning 'winding') would have provided a natural corridor. This canal was dug for about half a mile towards Exwick, from a point known as Flowerpot, but canal mania waned and the project was abandoned. It is unlikely that Exwick will ever experience the terrible floods it has endured in the past as the various flood prevention schemes seem to cope with any excess waters.

This large drainage dyke helps to prevent flooding and provides a facility for model power boats, fishing and windsurfing.

Lower Exwick Mill was originally Hitchcock, Maunders and Co., who were woollen manufacturers, and its workers probably drank at The Lamb Inn, now The Village Inn. For a short while it was run by the extremely popular former Exeter City footballer, the 'tigerish tackling' John Delve.

ST THOMAS

St Thomas 'enjoys' something quite rare in Devon, a flat site. Spread over the lowlands between the River Exe and the base of Redhills, this 'town' within a city has its own identity.

St Thomas Church and the Famous

There is almost something biblical about the chosen site for the current St Thomas Church, it being built on much more firm ground than the original church. According to an old newspaper cutting: "The ancient church was situated in a swampy place, and so near the Exe, by the road towards Whitestone, and was so subject to inundations that the parishioners petitioned the bishop for a removal of it. It was pulled down soon after the Reformation; when the present church was built in its stead, in a more eligible situation."

One of the great Victorian heroes paid a visit to St Thomas Church, on an occasion when his life took a dramatic turn. General Gordon had served in the Crimean War, seen action in China and Egypt and had spent the years 1877–79 in Sudan where, as Governor, he tried to suppress the wheelings and dealings of the slave trade. Following this he travelled widely, visiting such diverse places as Ireland and India before returning to England.

He came to Exeter to visit his friend the Preb. R. H. Barnes at Heavitree Vicarage. Whilst there he made a pilgrimage to visit St Thomas Church as he wanted to make a first visit to his grandfather's tomb which was within it. However on arrival the great General came face to face with a firmly locked church door. Not to be thwarted he sent somebody to get the key. Just as this was achieved, even as the key was inserted in the lock of the north door, a messenger arrived with a telegraph. The message summoned General Gordon to make immediate haste to London. From here he was to go straight back to the Sudan, this time to surpress the Moslem rebellion which had broken out under the leadership of the Mahdi. The rest of his story is, of course, well documented in history for the great man and his troops endured a ten month siege but just two days before relief arrived he was killed. A memorial, the Gordon Lamp, will be found in Heavitree but here in St Thomas the memory is one of his being so near, but so far from his paying homage to his grandfather.

There is a curious memorial, on the north wall of the church, to a heroine from the other end of the country. Grace Darling was the daughter of the lighthouse keeper of the Longstone lighthouse on the Farne Islands. On 7 September 1838, with her father, she risked life and limb, during a storm, to row out and rescue nine men from a stricken steamer *Forfarshire*, off the Northumberland coast. There seems to be something of a mystery as to why she should be so specifically remembered at St Thomas, hundreds of miles from her native North East.

Emmanuel Church

St Thomas enjoyed a building boom in the last decades of the nineteenth century. In the period between 1881 and 1891 the population of these nether lands beside the Exe rose by a massive two thousand. This had its implications, particularly in a church-going society where a packed congregation knew that their little iron church was inadequate for their worshipping. There was a common will in the people so a second ecclesiastical district within the parish was created, the new 600-seater Emmanuel Church rising heavenwards as the nineteenth century reached its end. The land had been kindly given by Sir Redvers Buller, who was patron of the living of St Thomas. In response to the design specifications for a new church a staggering 113 sets of plans were submitted, the 'winner' being that of Harold Brakspear. The builder chosen to construct this Gothic design was Mr Nicholas Pratt, the well-known builder based at Clyst St Mary.

Redhills Hospital

An immense complex of buildings stands on the rise where Okehampton Road greets Exwick Road. I will always think of it as Redhills Hospital, a place where my amazing 'Nan' passed away some years ago now. It was only after she had been admitted that I ever knew what an impressive building it was. For better or for worse it has now become a residential area. When you look at the poor distribution of secondary schools in the city and see the strain on space for the St Thomas and Exwick districts you can imagine that a school built here would have solved a lot of problems! However, it's too late now but there are those who will live there unaware of the social history of the main complex of buildings erected in 1836–37 at the start of the Victorian era when Britain was Great (if you were wealthy).

The following extracts are from one of a series of articles written over a century ago about buildings in Devon, this being Number 11 and featuring our building, which started out as a Workhouse.

"This Workhouse, from its position within a few minutes walk of Exe Bridge, might fairly be enumerated among the public buildings of Exeter, just as the whole parish of St Thomas is popularly, although not officially, regarded as a portion of the town. This Institution ... is a place of refuge for the paupers of the fifty parishes of the Hundred of Exminster, all of which are rural except that of St Thomas.

As the City Workhouse, by its age and comeliness derived from the comparative liberality of its original builders, is distinguishable in appearance from Union houses in general, so the St Thomas Workhouse is saved from the cold and abject aspect of these institutions in many other counties, by the pleasing effect of the material of which it is constructed. Locally this distinction is less regarded, because, by the good fortune of the West, many of the cheapest structures are composed of those native grey and red geological lumps which are almost everywhere in the county easy to get, and, let the builder do what he will with them, almost as picturesque in architecture as in the gracefully rounded or broken hills from which they are taken ... The St Thomas Union House is ... cheerful in appearance. It is placed on the side of a hill, with the City of Exeter and the valley of the Exe for a prospect, and with the swell of green upland behind it, against which, as a background, it seems to lie as we approach it from Exeter. The fabric is of what is called Pocombe stone, from a neighbouring quarry, in equal-sided cubes. It is a composite material of red and grey, which, like all the hues of the Devon soil, blend pleasantly with the colours of pasture, orchard, hedgerow and wood. The Workhouse, taking a birdseye view of it, is a six-sided figure, inclosing a court, while the space inclosed is subdivided by three lines of building forming radii from the centre to the circumference of the hexagon, in the shape of the letter-Y.

... The entrance hall is the waiting room, furnished with seats for the accommodation of the applicants for relief. It is also the place where inmates see their friends ... and is warmed by a large patent stove.

... Back by the Board Room and entrance hall we proceed to the schoolmaster's private apartments, passing on the way a small comfortable room set apart for the chaplain. There is a broad, carpeted, staved ladder in the schoolmaster's sitting room leading to a trap in the ceiling, opening into the floor of the boy's schoolroom. By this means the schoolmaster, who cannot be accommodated with apartments contiguous to the school, has a very ready means of access to the scene of his labours, and when disorder reigns in the classes the apparition of his head and shoulders through a hole in the floor, like an imp in a pantomime must have a much more sedative and terrifying effect than if he entered the room, in a stale and commonplace way, by the door.

... Here are out-houses in rural fashion for storing coals, cleaning boots and so on. One of the apartments contains the private clothes, or rather rags, for the most part, which the paupers are found wearing when they are admitted into the house, docketed, tied up in tight bundles and placed on rack shelves. They are the squalid ghosts of the paupers' past existence, before the parish living is donned and a life of pure dependence is entered upon ... an unusually large proportion of the old clothes are the abandoned vestments of paupers whose labours are done and who have entered the workhouse to spend the remainder of their lives. Only a few of these bundles are ever required again."

The article, which could have filled several pages of this book with precise detail, painted an optimistic picture of the place which had a population of 223 paupers at the time it was published. The schoolmaster had the appropriate name of Canes, more than likely a verb in this instance! The Master and Matron were Mr and Mrs Timewell. There was a variety of occupations for the inmates, for those who were able-bodied, which included picking oakum, gardening, making mouse traps, shoe and cloth-making. It was interesting to note that there were forms of accommodation for different age groups and for those of married status. The article emphasised that there were facilities for the over-60s married couples to share living accommodation but that most opted to be in single sex dormitories rather than with their respective partners. The theory, as put forward by the Workhouse in the article, followed the old saying that 'Love flies out the window when poverty comes in at the door!' To gauge the size of the institution it was reckoned that to walk every inch of it would take about two hours.

Alphington Street

Alphington Street is now a very different street to the one it was years ago when it was packed with shops rather than dominated by Sainsbury's and the Riverside leisure complex. A read through past street directories will back up this statement, whichever year you look at, prior to the 'improvements' made to this street approaching Exe Bridges. The 1965 version reveals that the National Provincial Bank occupied number 1 Alphington Street, whilst Lloyd's were at number 2, and the Westminster Bank at number 15, with H. C. Evett at the helm. Going along the north-east side of that street, in those 'swinging sixties', were also Churchward the grocer, Wright the hairdresser, St Thomas Sub PO, Hill, Palmer & Edwards the well-known bakers, Stone the confectioners, G. Phillips & Sons (The Farmers' Friend), Lloyd Maunder the butcher, Badcocks Dairy Ltd, Floorcraft, Townsend the tobacconist, Roy the ladies' hairdresser, the Laundromat, Harding's Bakery, W. G. Shears the corn merchant, Smales Garage, Kerry's electrical wholesalers, the Royal Oak and Pike's garage. On the south-west side were more familiar names but less shops. However, older Exonians may remember the Plymouth Inn and the Buller's Arms, Hutchings fish and chip shop, Luxton's chemists, Knight the tobacconists, Eastman's the butchers, the Gun Shop, Beard's Bargain Stores, Sluggett & Son the butchers and Punchard & Son the printers. Harding's had a small baker's round van which used to visit Cedars Road, where I grew up, and I can remember gleefully buying stale buns and cakes at ridiculously cheap prices. I think the young lady felt sorry for me but I am paying the price now for all that calorific intake!

In the late 1940s and early 1950s Badcock's ice creams were apparently so delicious that queues formed all the way to Shooting Marsh Stile! About the same time, Bolt's dough cakes were also revered so much so that their 'yumminess' has survived some half a century or so in the memories of those fortunate enough to have sampled them. Oh happy days!

The Cattle Market – One Man's Meat ...

Since the first edition of this book the Cattle Market, which stood on the corner of Alphington Road and Marsh Barton Road, has relocated to the other end of the estate.

A modern shopping area, which features chain stores, now uses the site where the 'beef' once stood in pens, rather than in burgers like today! The cattle market had moved here, from Bonhay Road, in 1939.

It's Not Cricket!

As a child I can vividly recall watching some high profile cricket matches at the Grace Road ground of Exeter St Thomas Cricket Club. The ground was a pretty spectacle but the Marsh Barton estate was destined to eventually swamp it. Although the excellent, and enlarged club house survives, the 'pitch' has been virtually

swallowed up. However, a mural of Geoff Boycott, who played here, gazes out over the overgrown remains of the pitch towards the encroaching warehouses where once he stroked boundaries. Inside the building there are pictures on the walls of other stars who 'graced' this venue, in their prime in 1968, which include such great players as Clive Lloyd and Sir Garfield Sobers. The Duke of Edinburgh was another special guest in 1969. The nearest new road to this former ground is called Bradman Way (named after Sir Donald) and it's here the 'Jardine' (named after Douglas) industrial units have risen inside the old boundary rope. Good job they weren't stumped for an appropriate name or two!

One of the pictures shown here features the score board, now just a festering wreck, when it was another victim of those major floods of October 1960. The aerial picture bears some close inspection because it was taken at the same time. It also shows a much smaller Marsh

Barton. The railway runs across the picture and bisecting it on the left side is Clapperbrook Lane which then ran through green fields to Alphington. At the top right of the picture the route of the former Teign Valley railway can be spied, this before much residential development and before the A30 dual carriageway and Pocombe Bridge link road. How times change!

Villages Around Exeter

Exeter spread along the main routes which led into it mainly during the inter-war period. Far-off villages like Alphington, Pinhoe, and Topsham gradually witnessed that the countryside between them and Exeter was disappearing under an ever-growing jungle of buildings. The influence of Exeter upon these small settlements has been considerable. Yet there is a great deal of local pride still shown and it is this which helps to retain the identity of these communities.

IDE – The Village of the Lost Valley

Ide, although still outside the city limits, has been included as a personal choice because of its great beauty and for the many happy memories it holds for me. No self-respecting book about Exeter and its villages could leave out this beautiful village which sits snugly in a fold of the hills, sheltered from the worst effects of the prevailing winds. The steep hills above the village receive a plenteous supply of rainfall which creates many streams. This combination enabled the community to develop long ago.

To the north-east of the village is one of the three local pubs, the Twisted Oak which was, for many years, the Bridge Inn. Its previous name refers to the nearby bridge over the brook, and not the metallic merry-go-round that spans the main road. The presence of the road, and its unattractive attachments, has resulted in a memorial illustrating the feelings of some of the indigenous population.

Many people in Exeter will remember Mr Marriot who camped for years in the field beside the bridge. He led a spartan existence, frequently communing with nature in its most brutal moods. Surprisingly his choice of kilt, worn to Cathedral services and to the Exeter reference library, did not seem to dampen spirits. At the latter he stored a fine model of the former! He fought a prolonged battle with authorities before finally accepting alternative accommodation.

A College with no Students

The most photogenic feature of Ide is a row of cottages called The College. It was in one of these that I met several villagers who gave me much of this information about their village. Sadly, since that day in the autumn of 1981 many of them are no longer with us. The College was originally the property of the Church Commissioners, under the auspices of a collegiate church. It is possible in times of plague that priests from Exeter may have been accommodated temporarily to reduce the risk of them becoming victims. The College was once regarded as the poor and rough part of the village.

In front of The College is a stream, the Fordland Brook, which flows down to join the Alphin Brook at the Bridge Inn. A common sight is motorised vehicles travelling along the bed of the stream. It is said to be the second largest ford in Britain. The College is far less likely to succumb to flooding now as works above the village take away any flood waters by way of a series of pipes. These were put in as a negotiated feature by the canny Parish Council when the link road was built.

The Old Ide Burlesque Elections

In the first half of the nineteenth century, following a serious electoral contest for City or council representation, a further less official, burlesque election took place at Ide. The procession gathered at St Sidwells and marched proudly down Exeter's High and Fore Streets to the polling place on Ide Green. When some semblance of order was achieved a speech, which may have gone something like this, would have been made by one of the candidates: "My lords, ladies and gentlemen, I will promise that if returned for this borough (that is Ide!), it shall be equal to any place in the world; I will get His Majesty to reside here; both Houses of Parliament shall be built here; And that you may be able to have tea cheaper I will order a canal to be cut so that the largest ships from China shall come close to your doors; your mill stream shall be turned into milk; beer shall be pumped from your wells, made from the finest malt and hops that can be procured; I will order the adjacent hills to be opened for the supply of coals; free treacle will be supplied from the nearby Treacle Mine at Dunchideock; I will also have an Act of Parliament passed, that no widow shall marry before her husband's death."

You can imagine the cheering, jeering, booing and hissing that greeted such 'modest' election promises. At the end of the speech a show of hands indicated whether 'Lord Elpushall' or 'Baron Hardup' was to be elected, or not. The revelries continued long into the night with much noise and joviality.

Population

The amount of new building in Ide has been proportionate to its size. This has enabled the community to retain its village atmosphere even though the make-up of its population is changing visibly. Being so close to Exeter, the countryside and major roads, it is a prime location for growth. The number of houses in the village has increased but the population is still less than it was in 1851. This can be explained by citing the dilemma of a typical Victorian family, the Harris's, who lived near the Huntsman in a two-bedroomed cottage. Mother and father shared one bedroom whilst their ten children shared the other. (If half the children had shared their parents' room, the other half might never have come along!) Today the average household is small in comparison to the past but enjoys more living and sleeping space.

This picture shows Drake Farm in the heart of the village, which has been developed for residential use since it was taken in 1986.

Village Sport

Ide has never achieved any great sporting heights, probably through its lack of size. Finding a sports ground has been a problem for many years as the lands around the village have been utilised for agricultural purposes. Some of the fields which have been considered have been more suited to Association Mountaineering rather than soccer, whilst some of the meadows contemplated would have been better employed for water polo in the winter season. Years ago there was a field at West Town used for cricket but enthusiasm dwindled and the side declared. However, the re-establishment of a cricket team, in recent years, has resulted in a 'new' cricket pitch, set in the loveliest of surroundings, and once again it is located at West Town.

On maps made earlier this century a rifle range is shown above the village (SX 897 895). This was used regularly by the Army from a barracks in Exeter, but no evidence remains of it today.

The Ide Times

The free parish newspaper, the *Ide Times,* is delivered to all houses. It is paid for by advertising and social events. It informs villagers of all the various events and activities that are organised for them and helps to engender a healthy community feeling. The village is twinned with Canteloup Cléville in Normandy.

Bill Rowland

Since the first edition of this book I have continued my quest to know more about Ide. The man most responsible for 'putting me right' about the village was the late Bill Rowland who wrote a splendid book about Ide. Having lived there for a great many years he knew much about the village and was a source of information particularly to the many Americans whose surname was 'Ide' who came to discover their roots. There is also a type of fish called an 'Ide' which is found in lakes in southern Germany and which grows to about a metre in length, much bigger than the minnows in the Fordland Brook! Not a lot of people know that.

ALPHINGTON

Although now a part of Exeter, Alphington is three miles from it, or so milestones state. The village grew at the edge of the flood plain beside the Exe with the extensive marshes of Marsh Barton stretching away to the east. Despite avoiding floods from the mighty river the village has been inundated, on many occasions, by the waters of its own Alphin Brook. On 2 July 1760 a flash flood removed 20 houses and in 1960 a common sight was villagers struggling along the main street in rowing boats. This prompted the canalisation of the Alphin Brook and bravely (or is it foolishly?) several fine dwellings have been constructed where, at times, its flood-waters once formed lakes.

In 1645 General Fairfax realised the strategic importance of Alphington, and having routed the Royalists at Powderham, he made his headquarters there whilst he finished his plans for the Parliamentarian triumph in early 1646.

Charles Dickens

Despite living near the damp marshes longevity seems to be a feature of the folk who lived at Alphington in the past. In the reign of Elizabeth I a gentleman by the name of Stone is reputed to have lived until he was 120 years old. Perhaps this may have influenced Charles Dickens when he rented Mile End Cottage, from Mary Pannell in 1839, for his aging parents. A frequent visitor himself, the household included Charles' mother and father (Elizabeth and John), their servant, Hester Drinkwater, and 'Dash' their nippy little dog!

A Bank Holiday?

The beauty in compiling a book of this type is the freedom to include any odd anecdote, however unlikely or irrelevant, which takes the fancy. Such an event that fires the imagination occurred on 21 July 1669. Two hundred Alphington women donned white clothes and clean straw hats then, armed with mattocks and shovels, marched military-style to the accompaniment of drums beating, to the river bank – which they then repaired! No logical explanation is given for the ritualistic way in which this was done.

Alphington Horse Fair and Haldon Races

In the first half of the last century Alphington was famous for its cattle and horse fairs held close to the parish church. It was the largest horse fair held in Devon and people from all over the shire made their way to this village to participate. A great number of gypsies, expert in equine practices, attended whilst their wives added to their own fortunes by telling fortunes. To cater for the two-day long fair 23 public or 'bush' houses opened to provide liquid refreshment. The King William, the Double Lock, the Bell and the Admiral Vernon Inns all enjoyed good trade. At the latter, 60 geese were cooked to provide a feast for visitors. The last fair ceased in 1870 with many factors accounting for its demise, not least the growth of the railroads.

Early in the last century, every second week in August, Haldon Races were held on a Wednesday and Thursday. The main route to the races, from Exeter, passed through Alphington and many chose it as a rendezvous or as a place to get transport up to Haldon. Wagons and carts charged a shilling (5p) single fare, whilst donkey conveyance was half the price, with a stipulation that no more than three hours would be spent on the road – a journey of 5 miles. The event was so popular that from 4 a.m. to 9 a.m. a continuous line of people could be seen stretching from Exeter to well beyond Alphington. When the massive crowds returned to Exeter, later in the day, it was such a spectacle that many lady folk would make a social occasion of witnessing the procession. Many accidents occurred, especially with four-wheeled vehicles descending Haldon Hill, the cause being reckless driving!

Law and Order!

John Hele fulfilled his role of parish constable and postmaster as he was directly responsible for apprehending the law-breakers of Alphington, in the years either side of 1850. Amongst those sent down through his intervention was one poor youth who was transported to Australia for ten years for sheep stealing, and another who only got seven years for stealing apples.

John Courtenay Bonus made a more benevolent contribution when he died in 1936, leaving £200 to provide every poor person, of good character, with one pint of beer, stout or cider each Christmas. This bequest surely reflects a man who lived up to his name!

Forward Planning

In the *Devon and Exeter Gazette*, dated September 1929, Charlie Ross was angry about a newly-opened stretch of road from Alphington Church to Matford (SX 929 892). He referred to the folly of opening a switchback route with hairpin bends and steep gradients. He cited the death of a motor cyclist, a few months earlier, and gave vent to his feelings that this was an avoidable incident. In his opinion planners should have taken the route to the north-east of Knowle Hill as this would have provided a more level gradient and no bends. His proposed route of 1929, to relieve Marsh Barton and Alphington of its heavy traffic, was not engineered until 1982, when the Matford link was opened.

Alphington Halt and Environs

The age of the train, for the village, ended in 1958 with the closure of the Exeter–Newton Abbot branch line via the Teign Valley. Alphington Halt was sited at Church

Road, and some picket fencing can still be seen beside the Alphington spur road to the A30 and a raised embankment is still visible. The railroad out of Exeter passed rows of Victorian houses, factories, tips and other unsightly scenes before reaching this tiny halt. Beyond, green fields and sylvan surroundings made a magnificent contrast. Two of my other books carry several pictures of this railway, these being *The Teign Valley of Yesteryear, Parts I and II*!

The railway bridge has disappeared as have the railings seen beyond it (now the roundabout). The cross shown was relocated beside the road. In the past an orchard stood where the corner of St Thomas School playing fields exists today. To deter would-be scrumpers, a wooden fence was constructed around its perimeter. This barrier took on an eerie appearance as several of the wooden stakes started to grow into trees!

The new roads have made drastic changes to the village. However, without them Alphington would be an endless nose-to-tail, dawn-to-dusk, traffic black spot. It is not beyond the realms of possibility that a true village atmosphere could be rekindled if the centre of the village was made a traffic-free or restric–ted area.

PINHOE

The 'village' of Pinhoe, 3 miles from the centre of Exeter, is now little more than a suburb. The former A38 Exeter–Bristol route initially spoilt its rural atmosphere and there are past pictures of nose-to-tail queues going nowhere fast through it. Even with the opening of the M5, partly an unofficial 'Pinhoe By pass', the village continues to see its fair share of through traffic on the reclassified 'B3181' (achieved by turning the A into a B and inserting a couple of ones!) The growth of Exeter and the attractiveness of a dormitory village so close to it has meant that Pinhoe has grown beyond recognition, particularly in the 1990s when the massive Monkerton estate, on the lower lands to the south of the village, was developed. This picture was taken in 1988 before the bulldozers moved in.But whatever the changes nothing can take away Pinhoe's colourful past ...

Pin the Tale on the Danes

In the year 1001 a battle between Ethelred and the Danes took place on the slopes of Pinhoe. Sorely pressed, a priest helped to relieve the situation temporarily by saddling his ass and riding in haste to Exeter to get a supply of arrows. Despite his brave efforts the Danes won. However, an annual pension of one mark was granted to the local priest and this has been paid ever since. One suggestion is that payment was made for offering prayers for the souls of the dead. Another more outlandish explanation says that when the priest was on his return journey from Exeter he was struck by an arrow which transfixed and ruined his hat; the allowance was thus meant to keep him in headwear. Local folk prefer to believe it was for the priest's bravery. Pinhoe's school badge depicts this event and the street names of Danesway and Saxon Avenue commemorate the spot where the battle took place.

Fire and Flood

These have played their part in shaping Pinhoe's history. In September 1925 six cottages, close to the centre of the village, were razed to the ground, rendering 25 people homeless. The nature of cobb and thatch when alight resulted in a conflagration that the fire brigade could not control.

Pinhoe's topography is clearly defined between the steep slopes to the north of the settlement, which are clay and poorly drained, and the lower areas, which are better drained and more gentle. The old A38 acts as an approximate boundary between these two areas. When storms break over the high hills above Pinhoe the rainfall is often so hard that it runs off the steep slopes and down into the village. This has happened many times, often with disastrous results. The 22 June 1933 storm was but one example of this phenomenon, with three Pinhoe families being rendered homeless. Three hours of violent rainstorms accompanied by heavy thunder and vivid lightning caused a deluge to rush down into the village. Bridge Cottages, near the railway line, were surrounded in water three feet deep. The residents retired upstairs but ominous sounds of cracking walls necessitated an escape via ladders. Church Hill was like a river, the water carrying immense loads of material with it as it rushed down across the main road and into Station Road. The flood was so sudden that residents did not have time to take preventative measures. The water was waist deep in the village centre, with manhole covers shooting two feet high into the air through the immense pressure of water in the drains.

School children were stranded at school, above the flood, whilst people needing to catch the train had little alternative but to improvise their state of dress and wade through the waters. Nearby Poltimore Park was turned into a lake for several hours. The waters quickly subsided and a fleet of lorries were called in to remove tons of stones, silt and debris. These events have been repeated but not with such fury or devastation.

The Village Hall

The community feeling of Pinhoe has been further perpetuated by its equivalent of a village hall, known as America Hall. Within this well-known building an immensely diverse range of activities take place from discos to whist drives, from playgroup meetings to gatherings of senior citizens.

The hall was built as a result of funds raised in the USA largely by Mrs Sidney de la Rue, whose efforts have received recognition in the name of the road leading to it. The hall is a thanksgiving gift for the kind way in which American soldiers were treated in Devon during the Second World War.

Tabitha Patch was heavily involved in raising the money for the site of the hall. Often single-handed, she arranged dances at the Temporary Hall beside the Pin Brook at Monkerton. Many of the teenagers who attended these events will recall that Tabitha had a way with young people. If their behaviour did not match her exacting standards she would take her stick to them and drive them from the hall. This stocky lady took no nonsense, but like so many of her ilk, was highly respected by all of the community. Many years later her son, Tony, very kindly lent many of the pictures which are featured in *Pinhoe of Yesteryear, Parts I and II.*

The Reverend Oliver Puckridge

Another great Pinhoe character who is still fondly remembered is the Reverend Oliver Puckridge. He is believed to be the last vicar to maintain the tradition of keeping a donkey. Oliver was a kindly, scholarly man who gained a degree at Clare College, Cambridge in 1881 and added an MA in 1885. He held 'livings' at Sourton, on the edge of Dartmoor, and at Sheldon before spending over 40 years at Pinhoe, arriving in 1902. His behaviour was regarded as eccentric. Typical was his scant respect for the laws of gravity when descending the very steep Church Hill on his beloved bicycle. He would swoop down the hill at an alarming speed towards the busy junction at the bottom. At the last moment he would veer sharply around the corner, onlookers hardly daring to watch. On one occasion when a member of the Royal Family was passing through Pinhoe the Rev. Puckridge raced again to the bottom of the hill, but this time with a step ladder attached to the cycle. As the Royal car approached he calmly put the steps up and climbed to the top. His ethereal viewpoint earned him an enthusiastic greeting from the Royal passer-by.

Rumour has it that when his donkey died a deep grave was dug for the animal. However, it was not quite deep enough and the donkey's ears were left poking out of the ground!

His memory is kept alive by the many villagers who remember him and a road is named in his honour.

Inns and Outs

Beside the railway bridge in Pinhoe is the Jubilee Club. This was built when Victoria had reached her historic milestone. The intention was to provide 'the working and sober man' with a place that he could adjourn to in order to read. It addition to the reading room was a meeting room where good teetotal conversation could flow. In recent years the club has expanded by adding many new facilities.

An older establishment is the Poltimore Arms, which was formerly the Bampfylde Arms. Apart from performing the obvious functions as a public house, other more unusual events have been held such as auctions of farm produce and reeds or withies. Until the turn of the century two of Pinhoe's main industries were basket making and thatching. The withies for these industries were grown largely in marshy fields to the east of the village, beside a tributary stream of the Pin Brook (SX 977 946). Withy Bridge is to the north of this poorly drained area.

A local legend suggests that one Lord Poltimore moved the pub from Poltimore to Pinhoe so that his labourers, who were strong cider drinkers, could attend church without being intoxicated. It was felt that this would stop them falling asleep during long sermons. The Poltimore family had connections with North Devon – there is another Poltimore Arms in North Molton.

In May 1863 the Clerk to the Trustees of the Exeter Turnpike Road, Mr N. Buckingham, wrote a letter to the London and South Western Railway Company about the new railway bridge at Venny Bridges in Pinhoe. It said: "... that the said trustees apprehend danger to the passengers on such road in consequence of horses being frightened by the sight of engines or carriages travelling up the railway ..."

The letter enquired about what measures the railway company were going to do to alleviate or lessen such dangers. The reply is not known.

The railway grew in local importance with Pinhoe Station at one time employing 13 men. The photograph reveals a complex of buildings which is in stark contrast to the scene today. This was originally a one-storeyed signal box which was enlarged to accommodate the station master whilst a new signal box was built beyond Station Road. The redundant signal box was loaded onto a lorry and carried to Bere Ferrers station, in the Tamar Valley, where it stands beside the Tamar Valley branch line. Another long-gone artifact, the former station footbridge, was believed to be the first prestressed concrete bridge used on this railway.

Saw Pits

Teams of sawyers travelling around the countryside had three venues in Pinhoe where they could set to work. The three saw pits were marked on old maps, two being at Monkerton and the other at the top bend of Langaton Lane. The 'under dog' strained for dear life in the bottom of the pit to wield the saw back into position whilst the 'top dog' straddled the pit to negotiate the act of sawing the timber.

The Exeter By pass

The Exeter By pass runs from the edge of Pinhoe around the former edge of Exeter. It was intended to be a quick route but for different reasons, at different times, it has been a highway dogged by traffic delays. Today it is a stop/go affair and is no longer the freeway that it was intended to be. All along its length there has been change, green fields giving away to development. Supermarket giants – Sainsbury and Tesco – business parks, schools, residential areas, and so on have all added to the load of this overworked road. Each new conglomeration has meant a junction and a set of traffic lights, always ready to turn red as you approach!

The hut encampment of Hele's School (St Peter's) has gone but it was no great visual adornment to the landscape, although there are those who will have fond memories of cold winters, and 'interesting' lessons, spent there.

The Digby development, following in the wake of the great deinstitutionalisation epoch, has changed the face of the former 'asylum' and one of the biggest buildings in Devon now provides new creature comforts and residents even have a 'new' railway station on their doorstep. One resident displayed a sticker in her window saying "You don't have to be mad to live here ... but it helps". Is this a good example of irony? Somebody also wrote to me and suggested that I write a book, a sequel to this one, about all the disappearing institutions of the Exeter area, which would have included Exminster, Wonford and Western Counties at Starcross. He also furnished me with a title – 'The Lost Marbles of Exeter' – but really it is the loss of green fields under the relentless regime of turning the city's rural fringe into one large residential, industrial and business zone, a small version of south-east England, a megalopolis, and that is not an appealing prospect. It is not surprising to note that every green-field site on this side of Exeter has attracted the eye of the predatory speculator.

TOPSHAM

Exeter now includes Topsham within its boundaries but don't tell the genuine Topsham local! If you have never explored, or been on one of the guided walks around the nooks, side streets or many pubs of Topsham then you have missed a real treat.

The waterfront, which gives Topsham its real character and charm, has obviously seen change but is still well worth a visit. On a warm summer evening the scene is serene, people 'messing about in boats' or sitting in a beer garden at the water's edge. One can enjoy panoramic views across the whole range of the Haldon Hills from the obelisk at Mamhead to the satellite tracking station at Waddles Down above Whitestone. A sunset, from places like the church steps, is a joy to behold.

The Changing Waterfront

Industrial archaeologists can tax their brains in examining the buildings along the waterfront as many have changed their functions, losing their ties with the sea, in favour of providing accommodation. Nail Cellars and Nail House in Ferry Road were purchased in 1858 by the grand-sounding Wigzell's Patent Spiral Fluted Nail Company Limited! Alas, its trade was more short-lived than its name, closing in 1861. Since then the building has been the West of England Wagon Works, a Salvation Army Meeting House, a rifle range, a coal store and a Church Institute. Nearby a three-storey block, formerly the site of Woolcomb's Sailmakers, is faced in unmistakable Hurdwick or Tavistock Stone.

The Lighter Inn derives its name from the small flat-bottomed boats called 'lighters' which were used to unload larger ships that could not negotiate the shallower approaches to Topsham harbour. This was originally the Customs House. However, it would be impractical to attempt to catalogue all the waterfront changes. Why not go to Topsham and be prepared to wander around the waterfront back alleys to see the changes for yourself or even, better still, go on one of the guided walks that are organised on certain days.

Topsham's Sea Links

Topsham today is incognito as a port for it has garlanded the waterfront in all manner of obstacles to prevent a clear portrait of what it was like in its heyday, during the seventeenth century, when possibly it was the second busiest port of England. Flats appear where cargoes once stood high, garden walls obscure old limekilns, whilst other alterations have cosmetically removed the formerly immense maritime connections of the waterfront buildings. From the Recreation Ground, a field reclaimed from a swamp, down to Riversmeet was a succession of quays, docks, boatyards and slipways. To supplement this were warehouses, stores, workshops and places which made everything connected with the sea: winches, chains, anchors, ropes, nails and sails. Nestling in on this hive of industry came those with a vested interest – the merchants and the mariners.

Despite the diminutive size of the vessels which plied the seas out of Topsham, trade was carried on to far-off places like Newfoundland, Charlestown and Nova Scotia. A lion's share of the trade was with European ports. Fruit and wines were imported from France whilst wool was traded with Holland and Germany. In the past, other items imported were wheat, linen, hemp, flax, olive oil, shumack, argol, cochineal, indigo, logwood, rags, tar, pitch and iron.

Many dignitaries who sponsored trade had large country mansions near the town. At Newport, on the northern fringe of Topsham, the D'Urban family achieved immortality, in name, as Durban in South Africa is named after Sir Benjamin D'Urban.

Another unusual export was people. These were the poor villains who were sentenced to transportation to the penal colonies in Australia and in Virginia in the USA. Other exports included leather, paper, flour and firkins of butter. Vessels built at Topsham were schooners, brigs, barques, lighters and other small craft.

Topsham Ferry

Probably the shortest journey ever made out of Topsham is the one across the Exe to Exminster Marshes beyond. The ferry crossing has been strategically important for hundreds of years as an ancient trade route westwards, beyond the Haldon Hills, guaranteed it plenty of business. Earlier this century a family called Bolt operated the ferry. Their home was the nearby Passage Inn where they spent a good deal of time availing themselves of the obvious advantages of an inn for a residence. People requiring a ferry in those days would shout "Bolt" or "Boat". In various states of inebriation someone would stagger out of the inn and perform the required service. The ferry was one of the very few known to tack across a river whilst being rowed. Today it opens up some excellent walks for those interested in wildlife, as the Exe Estuary marshes are rich in species, Turf being favoured by those who prefer to seek refreshment.

The most grateful person ever to use Topsham Ferry must have been Captain Trankmore. One dark and misty night his voice hailed the ferryman. "Who is it?" called the ferryman. "Trankmore" came the reply. The ferryman adamantly refused to cross the murky waters to transport a ghost as Captain Trankmore had been lost at sea months earlier in a violent storm. Fortunately a braver person rowed over and delivered Trankmore back to his native town. It transpired that the wave which had washed him from his ship had carried him straight onto the deck of a passing Dutch East Indiaman bound the opposite way. The passing ships had not even seen each other!

Topsham on the Mud

When the tide is out the Exe Estuary is a muddy expanse. Its mud has been eyed on many occasions for possible uses. In February 1853 Henry Phillips of Clyst Honiton made a few dozen bricks from it. Thus the 'Topsham Brick and Tile Company' was planned to gainfully employ those poor unfortunates without work. These words launched this venture: "We hail, with much pleasure, the completion of bricks made from Topsham mud which turn out to be first rate, sample and quality, fit for the finest buildings."

The hope was to extend this to tiles and pottery. The company's progress is not known and it must be assumed that the tide turned on their fortunes.

However, a recreational use of the mud has been made during the weeks of the town fair. Soccer matches played on the mud, which is a few feet thick and soft, finish with all participants crusted in a generous coating of mud.

When Topsham's famous mud is not on show the estuary assumes the appearance of a large lake. The shallow waters, rich in food resources, attract many fish and a wide variety of birds. This in turn attracts both commercial and recreational fishermen as well as ornithologists. The number of licences issued for salmon fishing is strictly limited. Many of the old fishermen reflect upon the catches that took place in the past. Their young sons, nephews and colleagues struggle on in the season to supplement their income. The day of the full-time fisherman in Topsham is long gone.

Goats Walk

Beyond the Strand is a wall, built about 1912, which gives a dry passage alongside the estuary towards Riversmeet and the Bowling Green Marshes. This thoroughfare,

about five feet wide, yields marvellous views in most directions and is called Goats Walk. Apparently at a Council meeting, which was arranged to adopt a name for it, one of the older and wiser locals boldly said, "It bain't be a road, it be more of a goat's walk." He wasn't kidding – that's how it got its name, Topsham fashion.

Workaday Topsham

Until recent years Topsham was blessed with almost full employment. Even in the difficult inter-war years most of the population were gainfully employed in a great diversification of pursuits. There were full-time fishermen, ship repair yards, a cider factory, many shops and even a manure store at Odham's Wharf. Travelling the streets were barrow boys selling fruit and vegetables, fish or rabbits. There were also five full-time milkmen using handcarts.

One of the biggest employers were the market gardens in and around the town. People always think of maritime Topsham but the land near the town is rich, red and fertile to the extent that it was able to support as many as 60 persons working it. The name which was famous in these pursuits was Pyne. Three families of Pynes known as 'Seabrook Pynes', 'High Street Pynes' and 'Denver Road Pynes' fought rigorously to corner the agricultural market. The last were regarded as the most successful as daily they loaded onto trains several cartloads of trees, canes, fruit and vegetables for Covent Garden. As everybody that worked for these nurseries lived in Topsham it was reckoned that the distant 'Seabrook Pynes' produced the best cyclists, whilst the 'Denver Road Pynes' managed to create the fastest walkers, of which Nippy Henson was a bionic supremo.

Apparently the workforce stopped for a half hour breakfast break at 8 a.m. 'Nippy' always walked home for his repast which, considering how far his Strand home was from the nurseries, meant that his walking speed was nothing less than sensational. According to those who remember, it was quite a sight to see him burning up the distance effortlessly.

At Smutty Harris's house, near the railway line, is a line of mysterious deep red sandstone cliffs which attract hundreds of geologically minded persons who come to gape in awe. Theories put forward range from former sea levels to Roman quarries. A marvellous 1:40 scale model of Topsham, housed in Topsham Museum, clearly shows the cliffs as a working quarry in 1900.

Smuggling

In a place like Topsham it must have been easier to be a smuggler than not. The narrow streets, warehouses, cellars, caves and hideyholes were almost custom-made for such antics. Newport Lodge, formerly known as Loggerheads Gate, was a celebrated smugglers' haunt. Many houses in the town contained specially constructed niches and stored all the items which were illicitly imported. Tight lips, stealthy movement and community involvement assured smugglers of free trade in Topsham.

Charities

The Topsham Consolidated Eleemosynary Charities (unpronounceable after a pint in each of Topsham's pubs), is an overall name for a collective number of charities in the town. Many have been amalgamated because the sums for endowment have been eroded by inflation. One charity which continues, does so only by courtesy of English law. 'The People of Topsham v St George's Hospital' was a case fought over the sum of £500 left by Mr Spicer in 1848. The hospital claimed the money for expenses when Spicer died, but the town won. The Market House Trust receives incomes from activities using the former Market House and redistributes the money for the betterment of the town: halls, schools, organisations, swimming baths and so on all benefit from generous gifts. Roy Wheeler has managed many of these charities and is confident that the people of the town are amongst the most generous in the land.

Some Topsham Notables Past and Present

Although this brief glimpse of Topsham is not intended to be a comprehensive guide it would be sacrilegious to omit mention of certain people who have shaped the life and atmosphere of this estuary settlement.

The Holmans are famous far afield for their great maritime past. John Holman masterminded the family's business development after 1836 when he left the sea, where he was a master mariner. This enterprising man started 'The Exeter Clubs' which was a mutual insurance scheme for local ship owners. John Holman and Sons was formed in 1850 dealing in housing, shipping and insurance.

In later years their stationery stated impressively that they covered almost every maritime requirement conceivable. They built barques up to 505 tons at Lower Yard and each was launched in style. A workforce of more than 300, plus dignitaries and the best local band, gave the vessel a fitting send-off. Following his death in 1863, the golden age of schooners, brigs and barques was soon to end. The larger iron vessels could not cope with the shallowness of the Exe Estuary and ship-building locations polarised towards larger ports with deeper approaches.

The Holman family moved their business interests to London in 1870 but despite this some members of the family remained locally. Dorothy Holman's Topsham Museum will give a much better insight into the Holmans' great past.

Two men who deserve recognition are boat builder Daniel Trout, and local independent councillor Morice Parsons. The former is a living legend according to many Topsham folk, an expert on the moods of the estuary. If there is any problem concerning local waters, the advice will be "see Daniel Trout". His boatyard is by the waterfront. Amazingly Dan, who has been harbourmaster for years and built many fine craft, cannot swim.

Topsham Wit

The funeral procession made their way into St Margaret's Church. The person making his last journey was a large man and had an outsize wooden overcoat. It was necessary that his coffin should be negotiated through the narrow belfry door, but try as they might, they could not enter. Having bruised his knuckles, the undertaker turned to the coffin and said, "We couldn't get you to church when you were alive, and we can't get you in now you're dead!"

Topsham Peculiarities

A soldier leaving a building at a hill station in India in the 1920s, left the door open. Immediately his superior sarcastically shouted after him, "Are you from Topsham?" Somewhat taken aback the young man had to reply, "Yes, Sir!" According to local legend, if Topsham Quay and Clyst Bridge are protected, Topsham folk need not leave their doors locked. Certainly, even today, many doors in Topsham remain open and many locals still forget to close doors when they go visiting.

Another controversy rages over the correct pronunciation of the town's name. Logic and local tongues refer back to the town's origin as Topa's Ham. Phonetically TOPSAM is the closest one will get to the correct form.

Another peculiarity of Topsham is the number of pubs in proportion to its size – all seem to enjoy a healthy trade as the estuary air is obviously conducive to a good thirst.

The former Railway Inn collapsed one Sunday evening in suspicious circumstances. A group of men had been playing cards and were shocked when one of their number bent down to pick up a card from the floor only to find his hand pinned down 'by the Devil'. A struggle followed and as the man escaped all the panic-stricken revellers fled the inn. An end wall of the Railway Inn collapsed almost simultaneously. The building was repaired but it was never licensed for spirits after that!

Many of the pubs have changed function. The Honest Heart became a drill hall and the Ship Aground became a baker's shop, birthplace of Morice Parsons, noted local councillor. Morice Parsons has served his town well, kept his eyes open to preserve that which is worthy and helped create that which is needed. This is a man who loves his town, as so many in Topsham do.

Buildings and Buyers

There is a bit of the roving architect in most of us and Topsham holds many gems. The building materials are varied; many of the grey 'brick' buildings are constructed of limestone which was brought by coasters from quarries handily located by the sea, at Berry Head and Babbacombe. Clinkers, which are flatter and smaller than English bricks, were brought by vessels returning from Holland and were often used as ballast. Indeed many of the merchant houses along the waterfront are regarded as 'Dutch' houses as they are copied from the style of gable found in the Netherlands.

Owing to Topsham's beauty and tranquillity it is a much sought-after residential area and has attracted, in recent years, people in a higher income bracket than its locals. The result of this trend is higher house prices and often local newly-weds have been forced to purchase elsewhere. However, Topsham-born people seem so proud of their town that they doggedly either attempt to stay, or vow to return as soon as possible.

Topsham Characters and Nicknames

It is impossible to have a town with such charisma without a multitude of colourful characters to ponder upon, albeit briefly. One of these is Roy Wheeler, who has lived at many different houses in the town having done much for the community as councillor, organiser and protector of the town's interests. He has also done many talks for Topsham schoolchildren and I am sure they are more aware of their heritage and history thanks to his efforts. We met on a few occasions to discuss what should be in this section of the book to portray a fair image of Topsham.

Nicknames are usually signs of popularity or familiarity. In the past almost every local had a nickname, many of them unusual. Some of the characters who remain on the lips of Topsham folk are: Nippy Henson, Bird's Eye Pidsley, Ranter Pym, Rocky Pilliphant, Farty Bray, Doc Sandford, Fishy Baker, Chuggy Amos, Fire Kennard, Uncle Matthews, Badger Luxon, King May, Acker Bowker, Army Harbottle, Fiddle Hurdle, Knowledge Voysey, Greaser Voysey, Nassie Wannell, Buckle Wannell, Pincher Pym, Long Pincher Pym, Small Pym, Goaty Edworthy, Twiss Edworthy and Lavender Boyce. Grand names for grand people!

Rocky Pilliphant, now presumably stoking the boiler of that eternal inferno down below, rode around Topsham on his bike with his small dog harnessed to it. At appointed spots in the town he would alight, daub some meaningful signs upon walls and then proceed to worship Beelzebub. Incantations would be readily served up at many different spots at different times of the day. People regarded him as totally harmless and took no notice of his hell-raising antics.

Perhaps he was influenced by a bizarre occurrence on 8 February 1855. A biped's hoof prints, in the snow, led in a continuous line over all obstacles from Exmouth to Topsham. It then continued from Starcross to Teignmouth mounting walls, roofs and all other obstructions. Through lack of any other evidence to the contrary, these are still, to this day, referred to as 'The Devil's Footprints'.

Chuggy Amos was another great protagonist of the bicycle. So attached was he to it that he even rigged up an unusual craft so that he could ride up and down the estuary, to the delight and dismay of passing yachtsmen.

Topsham Museum

The maxim that the best presents often come in the smallest parcels must surely hold true in the case of Topsham Museum in Lower Shaptor Street. It captures the

flavour of Topsham and has many interesting maps, models, photos and bric-à-brac to reflect Topsham's past. A fascinating scale model of Topsham as it was in 1900, complete with ships and shipyards, gives a real insight into the lay-out of the port. The museum was once a sailmaker's loft, which seems fitting. Visitors have been known to spend hours there, spellbound by the treasures which are housed, not priceless works of art but items which tell the stories of Topsham and its past. The late Dorothy Holman lovingly started this collection with the help and blessing of the people of Topsham.

Soccer on a Bowling Green?

The name of Pym is one of several which are synonymous with life in this settlement. Ranter Pym earned his name from bawling out his wares on the pavement. As a fishmonger it was necessary to be continuously vociferous in order to purvey his merchandise.

'Pincher' Pym (Dick Pym) is the town's most famous sporting son. He started as goalkeeper for Topsham St Margarets, was transferred to Exeter City and then on to Bolton Wanderers. With them he achieved an FA Cup winner's medal to reward him for a marvellous career.

The pitch on which he first began as custodian of the 'sticks' was called 'Bowling Green'. Nobody knows why this field should acquire such a name. It is located close to the confluence of the River Clyst and Exe and was once beneath the waters of the tides. In the 1840s a group of unemployed persons built a bank around the water's edge with a view to utilising the land. It became, in time, the home of the football team but unfortunately had no changing rooms. On match days teams changed at Eli Pring's 'Lighter Inn' before making the relatively long journey along the Strand, the Goats Walk and eventually to Bowling Green. The home team used bicycles, whilst the visitors either walked or re-embarked upon their conveyance to drive there. The poor referee had to walk to illustrate his impartiality. If well-supported Topsham lost, his journey back along the narrow Goats Walk, adjacent to the estuary, was a perilous one – Topsham had a great home record! The team had a lot of success when Topsham Barracks (latterly Wyvern Barracks) in Topsham Road, Exeter provided many good players.

Topsham Barracks was so called because Topsham's boundaries once extended as far as the County Hall in Exeter and the barracks were sited on land belonging to the town. The growth of Exeter absorbed the whole of the Countess Wear area. However, should you telephone anyone in that area, you have to dial the Topsham code first. The local boundary, on the Exeter side, is now at Newport Lodge, although, as mentioned earlier, officially Topsham is a part of Exeter.

If you want to know more about this estuary village then you should read *Topsham Past and Present.*

The Leisure and Pleasure City

In a world of increased leisure and pleasure time it is interesting to look back at how Exonians were entertained in the past. Although the City has rarely attained great sporting heights, it has had its moments. This brief look features some of the highs and lows of Exeter's social history.

Exeter Theatres

It is thought that Exeter first had a regular theatre in 1348 but this seems unlikely as London did not have one until some 200 years later. Plays were supposedly held at 'Danes Castle', behind Exeter Prison, however, in the fifteenth century. A play about Robin Hood was performed each May Day from 1427 and fittingly the wealthy paid a king's ransom for their entrance whilst the poor made a token donation.

According to local legend the Devil lives in Devon. In 1749 at a theatre in Waterbeer Street, at a performance of *Dr Faustus* he made an impromptu guest appearance on stage beside an actor playing the role of 'Mephistopheles'. The audience ran from the 'house' and the players fled from the City!

Exeter's second theatre was built in 1787 in Bedford Street and its popularity caused the closure of the first one. Sarah Siddons, 'the Queen of Tragedy', was a famous actress who appeared in the 1789–90 season. She donated the profits from her last performance to the Devon and Exeter Hospital, a gesture which earned her even more devotees.

As many actors were eccentric and prone to exhibitions of irrational behaviour, some performances were not 'by the book'. In 1803 a company performing *Hamlet* drank more than their quota of ale, added many distasteful asides to Shakespeare's play, and were asked to leave Exeter.

In 1817 an attempt to install gas lighting failed and caused an explosion. Candles were then used for several years before gas lighting was reinstalled – only to ignite even more powerfully.

A decline in theatre audiences in 1818 was countered by attempts to provide more demonstrative performances. In a play called *The Woodman's Hut* there was a forest fire and trees fell liberally across the stage. One of the players suffered a broken ankle, another suffered a burst blood vessel. As these extremes failed to woo audiences back, the theatre closed and was surprisingly refurbished more luxuriously in 1819. Alas, a year later a fire on 8 March did extensive damage but no loss of life was sustained. Perhaps the Devil was taking a curtain call!

The third theatre thus replaced the second on the same site and shortly after its opening a dramatic incident occurred, when in an attempt to recreate authenticity a horse-drawn vehicle appeared on stage, the musicians 'struck-up', the horse reared and it reversed into the stage lights.

Towards the end of the nineteenth century the theatre attracted less sophisticated audiences and adapted by providing less cultured productions. Its decline was again rudely halted by fire on 17 February 1885, which gutted the theatre completely, the cause unknown.

The Theatre Royal Disaster

There cannot be many true Exonians who do not know the fate of the Theatre

Royal, the fourth theatre in Exeter, opened on 13 October 1886 at the junction of New North Road and Longbrook Street. Less than a year after its opening it was also burned out, killing 188 people, and is still listed in the *Guinness Book of Records* as 'the highest death toll in a single building in the UK'.

'An entirely new and original romance' was being played by Gilbert Elliot's company. *Romany Rye* was into its fourth act on that fateful Monday night with about 800 persons being entertained. At 10.10 p.m. a character called 'Scragger' was left alone on stage when he was interrupted by the drop scene crashing to the floor.

As one might imagine, this sudden, unscripted event brought spontaneous laughter but within seconds this was transformed into immediate horror as the front rows of the house caught sight of a blazing stage. Most of the audience made an easy exit amongst the obvious chaos and confusion. It was the poor people who were unfortunate enough to have been in the Gallery who had little chance of escape. Their one exit was down a dark narrow staircase, poorly lit even in normal circumstances. Even this weak lighting failed, so when a child fell to the ground the panic-stricken theatre-goers ignored her plight and pressed on regardless, piling on top of each other. Most of those who died were not burned but expired through suffocation in the one-yard-wide passage.

Most of the dead were from the 300 or so theatre-goers seated up 'in the Gods'. To extricate these poor people many deeds of bravery were attempted. William Hunt, a sailor, climbed monkey fashion up the sheer-sided brick pillars at the front of the theatre and saved more than 20 people by bringing them down on his back. A policeman also rushed into the theatre many times, and amongst the people he rescued was his own wife. Bombardier Scattergood also performed many heroic deeds in the fire but sadly became a victim of the holocaust.

Naturally the various local fire brigades did their best. Their enthusiasm and dedication is summed up by the Topsham brigade which spotted the flames leaping high in the night sky. So as not to waste precious time, they set off pulling their tender by hand. It was not until they had got as far as Countess Wear that a fireman caught them up with a horse to tow it on into Exeter!

The following morning the horror of the disaster was most obvious. At the nearby former London Inn the charred corpses were laid out in the yard and stables and relatives tried to identify the bodies. In the shell of the building 50 bodies had been found piled up against the ticket box which had toppled over. The metal ash trays on the backs of the seats had melted through the intense heat of the inferno. The easiest bodies to identify were those who had jumped over 40 feet from outside balconies onto the pavement below.

After every disaster, fingers point accusingly and this was certainly the case in Exeter as many looked to the architect, Mr Phipps, and then to the magistrates who granted a licence to such an ill-designed place of entertainment. As 98 children were orphaned by the fire an appeal was made which realised more than £20,000, and this included a donation of £100 from an aging Queen Victoria.

If there had been an iron safety curtain, if the stage had been lit by electricity, if the gallery had been wider, then the disaster might have been avoided. As a direct consequence of this, regulations were introduced which were enforced globally.

The Theatre Royal, after further repairs, reopened with many of the world's great performers later appearing on its stage despite a general decline in theatre audiences. Shows like *Annie Get Your Gun* and *Brigadoon* were put on by touring West End performers. The Saddlers Wells Ballet and travelling circuses both performed on the large stage (but not at the same time!). One of the rare times a show was cancelled happened when a touring ice show arrived late to find that their stage, 10 cwts of crushed ice, had melted! Other stars who visited the Theatre Royal on their way to stardom included Morecambe and Wise and Val Doonican.

It also acted as a cinema for several years but as its 1,500 seats were rarely filled the building declined in popularity. I remember being taken to see the stage play of *Doctor at Sea* which starred a young Richard Briers. This was shortly before it closed in 1962. The site is now occupied by an insurance building – I hope it is covered against fire!

Cinemas in Exeter.

The first moving pictures seen in Exeter were displayed by travelling showmen early this century. 'Poole's Myriorama' made frequent visits to the city but it was 'West's Animated Pictures' that captured the imagination of the public. Victoria Hall was the venue for these pictures, shown by means of rollers projected onto elaborate canvasses. The audience were invited to choose their entertainment from a selection of 50 offerings. Most of the material enabled the audience to experience situations which were foreign to them. 'Shooting rapids, entering erupting volcanoes, experiencing huge storms at sea and riding on the footplate of high speed steam trains' earned Mr West rapturous applause from enthusiastic audiences.

The Victoria Hall was located in Queen Street at a point where untimely railway engines would emerge from the tunnel and spoil a sensitive piece of music. This was a constant occurrence in a theatre which was a scaled down version of the Albert Hall in London. Ironically it, too, was destroyed by fire following an evening when a railway company had hired the hall.

A travelling bioscope show accompanied Anderton and Rowland on their Westcountry travels. These were staged in canvas booths fronted by strikingly ornate screens. Wild West Acts dominated the show, accompanied by a large organ and dancing girls. Moving picture shows were added to this bill and boosted audience numbers. Other film exhibitions in Exeter included regular Easter shows in Kerswell's Field at St Thomas.

The first cinema, the Empire Electric, was opened in 1920 at the expense of a restaurant. A proud boast etched above the paybox proclaimed "You know one half of the world, we show you the other". Silent films shown at the Empire were accompanied by 'Miss L' whose sessions of playing the piano spanned eight hours of 'entertainment'. All this time she toiled to reflect the mood of each scene in the smoke-filled auditorium. She was positioned so close to the screen that she had to crane her neck at such an angle that certain stiffness and discomfort must have been felt. Mr W. A. G. Phillips, in an article which appeared long ago in the *Express and Echo*, stated that as a youngster he imagined that 'Miss L' had a life of bliss. She was able to sit and watch the pictures, free, for many hours whilst amusing herself playing the piano – and she was actually paid for doing so!

The next cinema to open was the Franklin Picture Palace situated at the top of Fore Street, almost opposite the Mint, in the Assembly Hall of the Franklin Hotel. Despite specialising in showing Charlie Chaplin movies, this small cinema had a short life and closed in 1923.

A humble grocer's shop became Exeter's most successful cinema in 1912. The City Palace was backed by many well-known business men and its popularity was largely responsible for the rise of King's Hall in Okehampton Street, now a night-club overlooking the river. Although built at an earlier date, the King's Hall's life as a cinema began in 1921. Eight years after its opening it pioneered the showing of 'talkies' in Exeter. This was less than a year after such movies had been witnessed in London, proving that Devon was not as remote as many 'up country' folk were led to believe.

Two other cinemas which existed in the 1920s were the Plaza and the Palladium. The latter was in Paris Street and originally known as Queen's Hall. It attracted people for dancing and variety shows in the 'good old days' before the movies. The changing function of the Queen's Hall coincided with the change of name. The Hippodrome (now the site of Boots in the High Street) followed suit in a similar adaptation.

The 1930s was a decade of the super-cinema. In the bigger settlements like Exeter, the advent of 2,000-seater buildings meant that the so aptly named, and far less comfortable, 'flea pits' found it impossible to survive. In Exeter three gigantic cinemas appeared; these were the Gaumont Palace (1932), the Savoy (1936) and the Odeon (1937). Whilst these showed the latest films on the newest equipment to packed houses, the other smaller cinemas struggled. The City Palace (the Lounge), King's Hall, and the Empire fell swiftly by the wayside.

The Gaumont Palace opened on Whit Monday 1932, replacing a building called the Yacht Beverage, with a showing of *Sunshine Susie*. One of the films booked in its first year was *Frankenstein* which the city Watch Committee would not let anyone watch. Consequently bus loads of horror-stricken movie buffs travelled down to Topsham to see it there instead. Such parochialism still exists today, even though the Gaumont does not show films any more. Now it's a case of 'eyes down' as avid bingo fanatics utilise the former pride and joy of Exeter's first big cinema.

The Savoy (or ABC) in London Square, now the site of shops, had a colourful past, many stars having appeared on stage including the Rolling Stones and the Beatles.

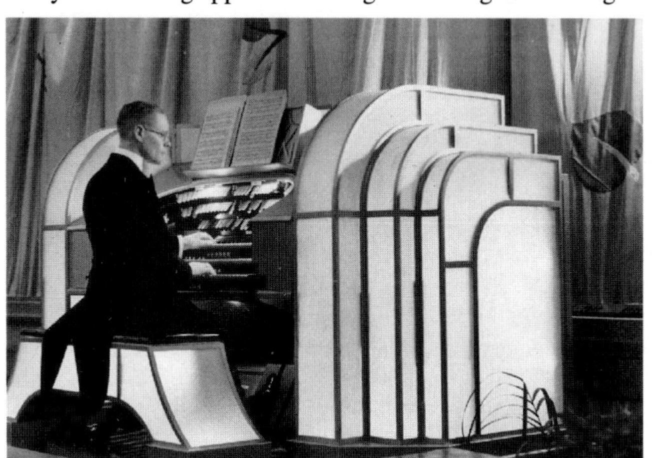

The most famous local person to appear regularly was the man with the big organ – the late Harold Stringer. During intervals he played a selection of popular tunes and light classics, accompanied by slide shows. At the height of the popularity of cinemas he would entertain almost 18,000 people each week. A sense of theatre was established by the dramatic entrance as the organ rose from the bowels of the cinema, lights flashing and most of the stops pulled out. The music was appreciated by cinema patrons and the media. Often the BBC transmitted Harold Stringer's concerts, which were at the zenith of their popularity in the 1930s and 1940s. The Gaumont's equivalent, 'The Mighty Wurlitzer', was destroyed in the 1942 bombing raids.

The Odeon in Sidwell Street opened in September 1937. Exeter's MP, Arthur Reed, Sir Edgar and Lady Plummer, were the celebrity guests. The first film to be shown was *The Charge of the Light Brigade* starring Errol Flyn and Olivia de Havilland. It was one of the first to show films on a Sunday, in November 1941, as some entertainment for troops on leave was seen as desirable. As Exeter is a Cathedral City there was naturally much opposition to this move. Councillor Ellen Tinkham vowed that if this happened "I shall resign my seat on the Council." And she did!

Since the Second World War there has been a general decline in the number of cinema-goers matched by a drop in the number of cinemas. The Gaumont, which had such a glorious past, no longer exhibits films. The ABC, in a bid to generate more custom, was subdivided into two smaller 'screens' with another part set aside for bingo but all this was to no avail and it was demolished in the 1980s. The Odeon has three screens, and carries on in an age dominated by 'multiplexes'. In 1996, the decline was halted with the opening of the plush, cosy 'Picture House' in Bartholomew Street West.

SPORT

The other form of entertainment which attracts crowds of spectators or participants is sport. Here is a brief study of the fortunes of just some of these sports.

Exeter City FC

Exeter City has a long history as a soccer club with many proud moments and whatever their status at the time this is being read, have had some good times in recent years. Here are just a few events and happenings for the record.

It was rugby which was first played at St James Park in the 1890s. Later Exeter United moved in to share the pitch. Not far away another group of enthusiastic soccer players known as St Sidwells United, whose home ground was at Monks Road, less than a mile away, joined forces with Exeter United. The two Uniteds united and dropped the United in favour of becoming Exeter City!

In 1904 Exeter played in the Plymouth and District League. Games with the local rivals, Plymouth, attracted only 50 to 60 people even though no entry fee was charged. Plymouth won the first derby game 2–0.

At one of the weekly meetings held at a local hostelry called the Red Lion it was decided to seek membership to the more prestigious Southern League. Sydney and Norman Thomas approached all the existing member clubs canvassing their support. In June 1908, at a meeting of the Southern League, Exeter were elected with a poll of 33 votes. Elected at the same meeting were Leyton (now Orient) with 32 votes, Southend 26 votes and Coventry City 25 votes.

Although red and white are the colours used by the City today, the team first appeared in green and white shirts and long navy blue shorts. The first League team to be entertained at St James Park was Bristol Rovers, the result also being a score draw. In that first season Exeter finished in sixth position.

An unusual circumstance arose if FA Cup replays were necessary in those pioneer years. As the playing surface at St James Park was smaller than FA Regulations, replays had to be staged at the County Ground in St Thomas.

After the First World War, the Football League added a Third Division, accepting teams from the Southern League First Division which included Exeter. A season later another league was added and the Third Division was subdivided into North and South regions. How Exeter City must have cursed their fortunes in 1933 when they finished runners-up, to find that only the top team got promotion to the Second Division. This is the nearest they have got to the upper echelons of the football world. By contrast they have reached rock bottom on no less than seven occasions, having to apply for re-election to the League in the years 1921, 1929, 1936, 1937, 1952, 1958 and 1961. Exeter City's best-ever Cup runs came in 1931 and 1981 when they reached the sixth rounds only to be beaten by Sunderland and Spurs respectively.

In an attempt to improve standards and make the League more competitive, the Football League changed the setup of the basement leagues. The top halves of the old Third Division North and Third Division South became the Third Division whilst the two lower halves formed the Fourth Division. Needless to say Exeter City dropped into the Fourth Division. Promotion was achieved in 1964 but the glory ended with a relegation some two years later. Life in the Fourth Division almost became a habit.

Before St James Park was a sports ground it was called St James Field. Travelling shows and circuses regularly gave performances there. It was common for great crowds to be entertained by many clowns. Some people might say nothing has changed but this does seem a little harsh!

Wrestling

This refers to the traditional form of combat and two notable venues were the Blue Ball Inn at Sandygate, on the outskirts of Exeter near Clyst St Mary, and at the courtyard of an inn in Topsham where championship fights of real venom were staged. Other fights took place in 1829 behind the Debtors Prison in St Thomas. This later became the site of the St Thomas Union Workhouse and after that Redhills Hospital but today it is a residential development.

Cricket

The late Bob Duguid remembered watching hundreds of barrow-loads of soil and earth being taken to the cricket ground in Pennyslvania. The frantic efforts of the helpers were made to get the ground ready for its official opening. The first person to bat on the new wicket was no less than the great W. G. Grace (1848–1915), who was out first ball in front of an extremely large crowd. The organisers, keen not to disappoint anyone, invited the brilliant Bristolian to bat again so that his immense ability could be appreciated.

Baseball

In August 1918 The National Cyclists Prisoners-of-War Fund was boosted by £50 when 1,500 people turned up to watch a baseball match at the County Ground. Although many of the crowd enjoyed the exhibition match, many claimed they would not wish to see it again as they did not know or understand the rules, a bit like Americans watching cricket for the first time!

Rugby (The Exeter Football Club)

Exeter Football Club played their first rugby match on 26 October 1872 at Millbrook, off Topsham Road, against the Training College (which later became St Luke's). Finding a home venue for matches was difficult in the formative years of the club. They played for six seasons at a field near the barracks in Topsham Road and moved to the Cricket Field, St Thomas (later called the County Ground) in 1882. Their stay was short-lived and they moved to Matford Lane where the club was supposedly 'invincible'. However, development speculators defeated them when they acquired the land for building and the club lost their pitch, which was close to the site of County Hall.

Unfortunately, when the team moved to the County Ground in 1890 they lost the county championship title. The next 20 years were difficult ones for Exeter and for rugby as a whole. Soccer became more popular and the crowds which followed the sport declined considerably, changing their allegiance to the round-ball game. However, those who continued to play rugby still 'enjoyed' matches like the regular fixture played against the United Services College, Westward Ho! The College always insisted that games should be played without a referee and afterwards provided a 'slap-up' feast for both teams.

In this era several players achieved not only fame on the field of play but distinction outside of the game. Two were Charles Tanner Kingdon Roberts, who became Mayor of Exeter in 1879, and his son 'Khaki' Roberts who played for England. After his career 'Khaki' was a prosecutor at the Nuremberg trials of war criminals.

On 16 September 1905 history was made at the County Ground when the New Zealand 'All Blacks' team played their first-ever match on British soil. Although the opposition was an unknown quantity it was felt that Devon, the County Champions, would come out on top. Six thousand people came along to watch, out of curiosity, and went away stunned and dazed by the revolutionary style of play which resulted in the All Blacks winning 55–4. Two of the New Zealanders amused the crowd, unintentionally, by sporting Panama hats to give them protection against the sun. When the All Blacks returned to their base, the Globe Hotel in Newton Abbot, they were given such a rapturous and warm reception that they made it their base for further tours. Devon's red faces were spared a little when the All Blacks trounced the Cornish 41–0 at Camborne five days later. In 1911 rugby football was played under gas powered floodlights supplied by Stansell's Acetylene Company of Exeter but rugby football overlords tended to frown on such fixtures.

The stand shown in the photograph was erected in 1894 but was burned down in March 1918 following a Service match. In the years which followed Exeter lost the

privilege of playing at the County Ground over a rent dispute. For a short while they played on a pitch behind Emmanuel Church in Okehampton Street before returning to the County Ground. In 1926 the stand which is used today was opened.

Throughout the years many of Exeter's players have represented England, or other home international countries. John Maxwell Batten, William Mann, T. S. Kelly, Dr J. C. R. Buchanan, P. M. S. Gedge, Sean McDermott, Henry Rew, Peter Candler, Alan Brown, Dick Mudge and Dick Manley are only a few of the stars who achieved international honours. T. S. Kelly captained England between 1906 and 1908 and often when he played for Exeter would run about 15 miles from his Tiverton home to the ground. Later he became a Customs officer in Exeter and maintained his ties with the club as Secretary.

During the Second World War the County Ground was taken over by American troops. The pitch disappeared beneath an assortment of tents as a great many coloured troops made themselves at home. The posts which supported the floodlights were supposedly chopped down and used as firewood. The quartermaster's stores for these troops were at the former Cattle Market on Marsh Barton. George Acton remembered finding 'goodies' at the bottom of his garden, adjacent to it – he presumed that the 7lb jars of jam left there were intended for the extremely attractive young lady who lived next door, but George didn't object!

After the war things returned to normal. The regular fixture with Exmouth on Boxing Day created one amusing incident. Play evidently got so heated that the referee called the teams together in the centre of the field and made them sing Christmas carols until the final whistle!

Exeter Football Club has the longest continuous history of any South-West rugby club: that is, providing you discount educational establishments. Along with the rowing club they are the only sports outfit permitted to wear the Exeter Coat of Arms. They also have the distinction of being allowed to hold Annual General Meetings in the Guildhall. The atmosphere there was so overpowering, however, that people were hesitant to voice their beliefs and the meetings stopped after 1932. The club still continues to have an affinity with Exeter and long may it thrive in the age of professional rugby.

Speedway

The thrills and spills of the dirt track have been seen in Exeter since 9 March 1929 when, in the first historic race, an Australian called Frank Arthur rode triumphantly to victory. Ever since, riders from all over the world have sped their way around Exeter's banked circuit.

The sport in this country began in the 1920s in spectacular fashion with 50,000-plus crowds regularly turning out in London. Even when Exeter opened, the average gate was a staggering 11,000 and this was maintained for many years.

The first racing near Exeter was at Peamore, handily placed at a point between Alphington and Kennford, where a small circuit staged meetings, using the same format, and also attracted large crowds. All the early events were individual competitions planned by the West of England Motor Club. In one meeting the legendary 'Harley Davidson' was used by one rider but the Bristol-built Douglas machine was the one favoured by most.

Gordon Taylor and Herbie Plain rode for the Exeter Falcons in the late 1940s. When they rode, in the company of such legendary riders as Bronco Slade and Cyril Rogers, the emphasis was more on skill and daring rather than sheer speed. By today's standards their times were comparatively slow but the racing was probably more exciting. In the 1940s Exeter's team progressed from the Third Division to the Second. However, in the 1950s there was a general decline in the fortunes of speedway and Exeter folded for a while before re-opening as a Provincial League outfit.

In the early 1960s I was a regular supporter when the team won almost every meeting at home but lost almost every meeting away. Riders such as Len Silver, Pete Lansdale, Alan Cowland, Dennis Day, Howdy Byford, Eric Howe and Francis Cann provided the thrills which entertained crowds of about 4,000 people. I can remember

watching several riders fall off in high speed crashes only to get up, dust off their leathers and get back on their bikes for a re-ride! This dangerous sport, however, has claimed many victims. Two Exeter riders killed on the track were Jack Unstead in 1961 and my old school chum, Tony Sanford, in 1981.

During the 1970s a remodelling of the league system resulted in Exeter being in the top flight of speedway racing – the British League. Riders such as Ivan Mauger put Exeter on the map as one of the best teams in the world. One of his many World Champion titles was in the Falcons' colours.

However, in a manipulative sport it is not uncommon for a track to close or acquire new status. This has happened at Exeter where, following changes in the league setup, the 'Flying Falcons' now race in what is generally regarded as the equivalent of a second division.

Cycle Racing

Another similar, but slower and less noisy sport which took place at the County Ground, for many years, was cycle racing. On Bank Holidays large crowds turned out to watch exciting events which drew participants from all over Britain, each hoping to win handsome cash prizes. One competitor who regularly 'stole' the top prize was a rider from Manchester called Brownlow. Each year local riders would vow to beat him but on the last bend he would always speed past towards rich pickings.

'Going to the Dogs'

The other form of racing to develop at the County Ground is greyhound racing, which started in 1929 and still draws punters who often go home with the tail between their legs. This sport started at Oak Marsh, Alphington (SX 913 904) when enthusiasts got together and organised races. Spectators passed through an improvised gate and paid a token entrance fee to watch the races. Today the same land is owned by the Newbery family of showjumping fame. The track then moved across to a much smaller and more rural Marsh Barton where a small stadium was built next to the railway bridge in Marsh Barton Road. From here the next move was to the County Ground.

And so, having explored many parts of 'The Lost City of Exeter', albeit in a roundabout fashion, we come to the end of this version of the book. Change is an on-going process and even as you read this book someone or something will be changing: new houses, offices, business parks, one-way systems, traffic-calming measures, demolitions, 'evacuations', people passing on or through, and so it goes inexorably on. I hope you enjoyed this look at Exeter and despite the change, it's still the most wonderful place in which to live!